GOING BEYOND AID

For decades developing countries have been trying to catch up with industrialized high-income countries, but few have succeeded. Historically, structural transformation has been a powerful engine of growth and job creation. Traditional development aid is inadequate to address the bottlenecks for structural transformation, and hence is ineffective. In this book, Justin Yifu Lin and Yan Wang use the theoretical foundations of New Structural Economics to examine South-South development aid and cooperation from the angle of structural transformation.

By studying the successful economic transformation of countries such as China and South Korea through "multiple win" solutions based on comparative advantages and economy of scale, and by presenting new ideas and different perspectives from emerging market economies such as Brazil, India, and other BRICS countries, the authors bring a new narrative to broaden the ongoing discussions of post-2015 development aid and cooperation as well as the definitions of aid and cooperation.

DR. JUSTIN YIFU LIN is Director at the Center for New Structural Economics, Dean at the Institute of South-South Cooperation and Development, and Professor and Honorary Dean at the National School of Development, Peking University. He was also formerly Chief Economist and Senior Vice President at the World Bank.

DR. YAN WANG is currently Visiting Professor at George Washington University and Senior Fellow at the National School of Development, Peking University. She was senior economist at the World Bank for 20 years before retirement.

Going Beyond Aid

Development Cooperation for Structural Transformation

Justin Yifu Lin

Peking University

Yan Wang

George Washington University

CAMBRIDGE
UNIVERSITY PRESS

CAMBRIDGE
UNIVERSITY PRESS

University Printing House, Cambridge CB2 8BS, United Kingdom

Cambridge University Press is part of the University of Cambridge.

It furthers the University's mission by disseminating knowledge in the pursuit of education, learning, and research at the highest international levels of excellence.

www.cambridge.org
Information on this title: www.cambridge.org/9781316607152
10.1017/9781316597354

First published 2017

Printed in the United States of America by Sheridan Books, Inc.

A catalogue record for this publication is available from the British Library.

ISBN 978-1-107-15329-5 Hardback
ISBN 978-1-316-60715-2 Paperback

Contents

Figures

Tables

Boxes

xiii

Preface

This book is motivated by our desire to help the world's poor benefit from development assistance from developed and emerging countries. Justin Lin, the first chief economist of the World Bank from the developing world, made numerous trips to developing countries, including more than 30 visits to sub-Saharan countries during his World Bank tenure (2008–2012) and thereafter. In those trips, he had the privilege of meeting with heads of state, ministers, intellectuals, entrepreneurs, and common people in the developing countries and gained a deep understanding of their aspirations. Yan Wang was the research coordinator of the OECD–DAC and China Study Group, and a World Bank senior economist. She also traveled frequently to Africa and other developing countries, interviewing many policy-makers at the minister or director levels as well as business executives. We both understood, through these personal interactions, their commonly held desire – a dream for a better future for their countries and people through their own efforts. Their dream is essentially the one we have had for China for centuries. Hence this book.

We would like to thank all those who provided inspiration and supports during the process of our learning and developing of ideas related to this book. In particular, we have benefited from inputs and comments by Pieter Bottelier, Deborah Braütigam, Richard Carey, Chuan Chen, Jason C. Cheng, Kevin P. Gallagher, Zhongxia Jin, Naohiro Kitano, Margaret McMillan, Célestin Monga, Manzoor Rehman, Joseph Stiglitz, Xiaoyang Tang, Jiajun Xu, Douglas Zeng, and three anonymous referees.

All the tables and charts were produced by several research assistants at George Washington University, where Yan teaches. We thank them – Chunxu Chen, Eiji Goto, Nan Hu, Haixiao Wu, Murong Xin, Feng Zhang, and Virginia Zhang – for their excellent work. All errors and omissions are our own responsibility.

We would also like to thank Bruce Ross-Larson and his team at Communications Development for their excellent editorial review, and Chris Harrison and Phil Good at Cambridge University Press for their encouragement.

Last and by no means the least, we are grateful for our spouses and families for their understanding, love, and support. In particular, Justin would like to thank Yunying, and Yan would like to thank Jeff and Virginia.

ONE

Introduction and Objectives

This book focuses on inclusive, sustainable structural transformation and its financing mechanisms because conventional development aid is inadequate to address the bottlenecks to growth in many developing and emerging market economies, including those in sub-Saharan Africa. In the next few decades, the development community and governments are going to focus on achieving the Sustainable Development Goals in 2030 and combating climate change as specified in COP21 objectives, both requiring huge amounts of resources. So, we need to go well beyond aid and purposefully combine aid, trade, and investment, using all financial instruments available and introducing new and innovative ones to meet the challenges of eliminating poverty and transforming industrial structures toward green and emission-reducing development. These tasks are daunting.

Aid, Trade, and Investment for Broader Development Goals

In today's increasingly dynamic, multipolar, and yet interdependent world, a new set of broader definitions of development finance – if applied – would improve the transparency, accountability, and selectivity of development partners. It would also encourage sovereign wealth funds and foreign direct investors, among others, to invest more effectively in developing countries and to support global and regional public goods. Indeed, that is what we do in *going beyond aid*. We offer multiple and more inclusive definitions than suggested by, say, the Organisation for Economic Co-operation and Development's Development Assistance Committee (OECD–DAC) (Lin and Wang 2014).[1] We also present future options and prospects for global governance.

Brazil, China, India, and other emerging economies provide not only new ideas, experiences, growth opportunities, and tacit knowledge but also financing for development. In the new multipolar world, BRICS countries, including China, are experiencing industrial diversification and upgrading, relocating their "comparative advantage–losing" industries to lower income countries and creating millions of jobs there. As newcomers, they are continuing to learn how to become better development partners and be more responsible stakeholders in global affairs. China in particular is also making a transition from a largely bilateral approach in development cooperation to supporting a multilateral system of cooperation.

Against a background of a plethora of recent initiatives – including the Asian Infrastructure Investment Bank (AIIB), the New Development Bank (formerly the BRICS Bank), the China-Africa Development Fund, the Silk Road Fund, and the South-South Development Fund – we hope this book will provide a framework for analysis and discussion to guide policies and practices for South-South Development Cooperation (SSDC). That framework combines aid, trade, and investment to achieve broader development goals such as employment generation and sustainable welfare improvement.

Why Go Beyond Aid?

According to the OECD definition, Official Development Assistance (ODA) includes grants and concessional loans (with a grant element of at least 25 percent) provided by governments and used for development.[2] The basic idea is that ODA must be concessional. Export credits do not count. Infrastructure loans, if not concessional enough, do not count. This definition, subject to strong criticism, has recently been revised (OECD–DAC 2014a). In our view, even the revised OECD–DAC definition is too restrictive.

Economic development is the main purpose of ODA, yet some of the more effective means of facilitating development, such as export credits and large but less concessional infrastructure investments, are excluded from the OECD–DAC definition. So this book goes beyond aid with a broader concept including trade, aid, and investment for development objectives, as long as those activities contribute to improving recipients' well-being.

One reason is that the main players in international development finance now include countries that are both *recipients* and *contributors* of such financing. As elaborated in the New Structural Economics,[3] the most effective and sustainable way for a low-income country to develop is to jump-start the process of structural transformation by developing sectors in which it has *latent comparative advantages*.[4] The government could intervene to reduce transaction costs for those sectors by, say, creating special economic zones or industrial parks with good infrastructure and an attractive business environment. If a developing country adopts this approach, it can immediately grow dynamically and launch a virtuous circle of job generation and poverty reduction, even though its national infrastructure and business environment may be poor.

We therefore propose a model of "joint learning and concerted transformation" where all development partners are learners on an equal footing, but are learning at different speeds. Learners at different stages of development can choose different learning partners (or "teammates") according to their own comparative advantages, "instruments of interaction,"[5] and degrees of complementarity. There is a freedom of selecting partners, development strategies as well as sequencing and priorities.[6] One learner could have multiple partners – upstream or downstream, North or South – each playing a mutually beneficial complementary role. Another analogy is that emerging and developing countries are at various stages of climbing the same mountain of structural transformation. In a globalized world, no one can climb that mountain without learning from and helping each other every step of the way.[7]

Brazil, China, India, and other emerging market economies – somewhat ahead in structural transformation – have many such instruments and high complementarities. For example, with a revealed comparative advantage in 45 of 97 subsectors, [8] and demonstrated capacities in building large infrastructure projects such as roads, ports, rail networks, and hydropower systems, China is in a position to provide ideas, tacit knowledge,[9] and help releasing the "bottlenecks" that prevent many developing countries from capturing the opportunities in structural transformation. And with labor costs rising steeply in China and other emerging economies, low-income countries can benefit from attracting labor-intensive enterprises that are relocating to places with lower labor costs (Lin 2012c; Lin and Wang 2014).

Importantly, our model is market-based one, based on "exchanging what I have with what you have," signifying mutual exchange on an equal footing. Following comparative advantages in trade and cooperation, both sides can gain from this trade, as we learn from Adam Smith. This could potentially align the interests of all partners – North or South, rich or not so rich, multilateral or bilateral – working together to try to reach "multiple win" solutions (Lin and Wang 2015).

A second reason this book goes beyond aid is that traditional development aid from the advanced countries has not been effective for poverty reduction, primarily because it was not used for structural transformation. If that traditional aid had been directed to augmenting the resources under the command of governments to ease the bottlenecks to growth in sectors with latent comparative advantages, it would have been better at reducing poverty and achieving inclusive and sustainable development in low-income countries.

Examples include improving infrastructure for special economic zones and building roads to ports.

In the past 30 years, China achieved the most rapid economic growth and poverty reduction – it alone accounted for most of the decline in extreme poverty over the past three decades. Between 1981 and 2011, 753 million people in China moved above the $1.90-a-day threshold. During the same time, the developing world as a whole saw a reduction in poverty of 1.1 billion (World Bank 2016).[10] Developing countries are looking at China's experience to see what has worked and how effective these policies are.

To end absolute poverty by 2030, international aid must be used in the context of other resources such as non-concessional loans, direct investment, and government spending (Development Initiatives 2013). Where aid is more effective – as in the Republic of Korea, China, Vietnam, and India – it has been used together with trade, foreign direct investment, commercial loans for infrastructure, bond and equity investments, and concessional or non-concessional export credit. Indeed, separating aid from trade and investment goes against market orientation.

A third reason is that South-South Development Cooperation would be most effective for poverty reduction in a poor country if it created a home-grown or local (not national) enabling environment for dynamic structural transformation in an economy characterized by poor infrastructure and distorted institutional environment. This solution to promote industrial clustering and agglomeration is more effective in low-income countries.[11]

A dynamically growing developing country is in the best position to help a poor country to jump-start dynamic structural transformation and poverty reduction: It can share its experience of building a localized enabling environment in special economic zones or industrial parks, and it can relocate its labor-intensive light manufacturing industries to the poor country in a "flying geese pattern" (Lin 2012c).

This book shows that South-South Development Cooperation from China and other emerging market economies is more likely to bring "quick wins" in poverty reduction and inclusive, sustainable growth. These economies, and especially China, have comparative advantages in infrastructure sectors, including construction material industries and civil engineering, fostered through grants, loans, and other financial arrangements, in a win-win for both sides. These economies, again China particularly, are relocating their light manufacturing, export-processing industries to low-income countries – industries in which the low-income countries have a latent comparative advantage. History suggests that any low-income country that can capture these relocating light manufacturing industries can have dynamic growth for several decades as it becomes a middle-income or even a high-income country.

The book also shows that Brazil, China, India, and other emerging market economies will, as newcomers, continue to learn to become better development partners and more responsible stakeholders in global affairs. "One cannot learn how to swim without jumping into the sea," as the Chinese proverb says. The new development banks and funds are steps in such a learning process.

Sometimes, emerging market economies need to be helped by other partners on social and environmental standards, safeguards, and risk management. Here, the international development community, nongovernmental organizations, and civil society come into play. All partners, in different positions in the development process, need to keep an open mind on South–North or trilateral cooperation, to ensure that it promotes "modern multilateralism." In a multipolar world, the emergence of new multilateral development institutions is inevitable and brings new momentum, energy, and competition to the development arena.

This short book does not attempt to cover all areas of foreign aid, nor does it present a comprehensive development framework, as foreign aid is closely related to the foreign policy of a country and wider issues of political economy. The book does not examine humanitarian aid, since that is guided by principles different from those of development aid and cooperation, nor is it an overview of China's foreign aid.[12] Instead, it studies the economics of development aid and cooperation from the angle of structural transformation, since ODA as currently defined and applied is ineffective for structural transformation (Chapter 3). It is time for the international development community to move on to new definitions that are broad enough to include multiple forms of SSDC, to facilitate triangular learning and cooperation, and to support low-income countries in capturing their windows of opportunity.

The Start of a New Era in 2015

The global development process seems to have reached a turning point. Never before did the balance of power shift as much as in March 2015, when 57 countries, including the United Kingdom, Germany, France, Italy, and many other European states became the founding members of the AIIB. More than 30 countries are waiting to join in 2016.

In our view, this shift represents a new era of globalization where southern countries are playing an increasingly important role. It also signifies a major change in China's development cooperation from bilateralism to multilateralism, as it deepens South-South and trilateral cooperation. Having experienced many frustrations in reforming the current multilateral development organizations, China is taking a greater leadership role in global development – forming multilateral financial bodies to reflect its development ideas, experience, and tacit knowledge. Building on many years of successful development, China is confident of the positive impact it can have on global development.

Nearly eight years after the global financial crisis broke, recovery is still anemic despite years of zero interest rates. The International Monetary Fund (IMF) adjusted downward the growth rates of all industrial countries in April 2016. Monolithic explanations of international development seem to fail in describing today's multi-polar world. Some world-renowned economists are discussing the possible "secular stagnation" of industrial countries.[13] Having lost confidence in the Washington Consensus[14] in the great recession, developing countries are increasingly looking to the East for experiences and ideas – for what has worked, why, and how.

China, based on its thousands of years of uninterrupted civilization and its recent 36 years of economic success, proposes a grand vision: "The Silk Road Economic Belt and the 21st Century Maritime Silk Road" (One Belt, One Road). It focuses on connectivity, infrastructure development, and structural transformation, with the AIIB and the Silk Road Fund as two of its funding mechanisms. This vision and new proposals by Chinese President Xi Jinping in September 2013 have won the hearts and minds of some developing and industrial countries, in Asia and beyond.

What is the rationale behind One Belt, One Road? We believe, first, that the vision reflects not only strong demand from countries overcoming infrastructure bottlenecks and improving connectivity, but also China's own key ideas and experiences for economic development. Building infrastructure sooner rather than later could facilitate trade at lower cost (Chapter 5). And building bottleneck-releasing infrastructure as a countercyclical measure could boost aggregate demand and long-term productivity. China has used expansionary monetary, fiscal, and investment policy to overcome contractionary pressures during two crises – 1998 (in Asia) and 2008–2009 (globally). The International Monetary Fund (IMF), after resisting for many years, has finally accepted the idea of building infrastructure as a countercyclical measure in a low interest rate environment,[15] and even recommends it (IMF 2014; See also Chapter 3, this volume).

We also believe that One Belt, One Road makes concrete the desires of Chinese leaders for "peaceful coexistence with differences" and commitments for providing global public goods, peace, security, and sustainability. China has provided development cooperation since the 1950s, when its per capita income was only one-third of Africa's. It has followed a revived Chinese value system of ren and yi (仁，义), which has rich meanings of several layers. One layer implies that "one wishing to be successful oneself seeks to help others to be successful; and one wishing to develop oneself seeks to help others to develop" ("己欲立而立人，己欲达而达人"). Another layer implies that "one should not impose on others what oneself does not desire" ("己所不欲,勿施于人").

These values were reflected in the Bandung principles of mutual respect and reciprocal non-interference, agreed at Bandung Conference in 1955, and they have been consistently implemented by China's foreign aid policy in the last 60 years. They will be modernized and strengthened by the current generation of leaders, as shown by the recent commitments to support global public goods and tackle climate change. "China now has its basic interest and responsibility in the systemic functioning of global development financing," as Xu and Carey (2015a) observed. As Chinese President Xi said in his interview in the *Washington Post* published on February 12, 2012, "The vast Pacific Ocean has ample space for China and the United States." In the same vein, our view is that the vast oceans are large enough to allow many developing nations to emerge peacefully – and that China's rise is conducive to world development and peace.

On the economic front, some of the considerations that motivated us to write this book are that

- Emerging and developing countries now account for more than 57 percent of global GDP; the advanced industrial countries account for less than 43 percent (Figure 1.1).
- In the 1990s, developing countries accounted for about a fifth of global growth. Today, emerging and developing countries account for two-thirds of global growth and are driving the global economy. China alone accounts for more than 30 percent of global growth. Given its economic size, 6.5 to 7 percent annual

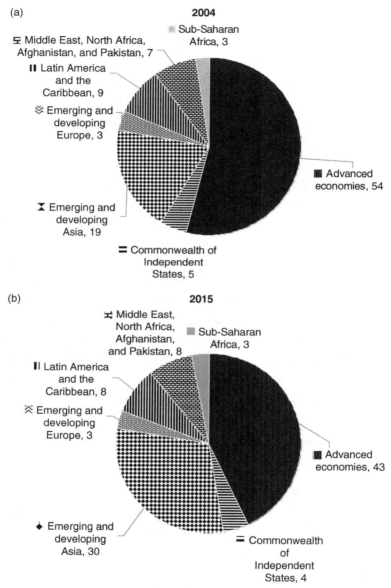

(a)   **2004**

Sub-Saharan Africa, 3

⊊ Middle East, North Africa, Afghanistan, and Pakistan, 7

‖ Latin America and the Caribbean, 9

⧹ Emerging and developing Europe, 3

⊼ Emerging and developing Asia, 19

═ Commonwealth of Independent States, 5

▦ Advanced economies, 54

(b)   **2015**

⊐ Middle East, North Africa, Afghanistan, and Pakistan, 8

Sub-Saharan Africa, 3

‖ Latin America and the Caribbean, 8

⧹ Emerging and developing Europe, 3

◆ Emerging and developing Asia, 30

═ Commonwealth of Independent States, 4

▦ Advanced economies, 43

Figure 1.1 Advanced and emerging and developing economies, 2004 and 2015
Source: IMF 2015.

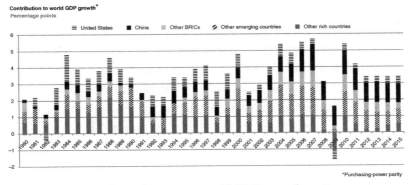

Figure 1.2 Contributions to world GDP growth, 1980–2015
Source: Based on IMF WEO data, with GDP growth at constant prices, and GDP based on purchasing power parity (PPP) as the weight, accessed September 7, 2015.

growth in China produces one-fourth to one-third of global growth (Figure 1.2).

- Over past 10 years, emerging economies have become major sources of international development finance, infrastructure investment, and outward foreign direct investment. The IMF finds, "In recent years, China has become the largest single trading partner for Africa and a key investor and provider of aid," and "a 1 percentage point increase in China's real domestic fixed asset investment growth has tended to increase sub-Saharan Africa's export growth rate on average by 0.6 percentage point" (IMF 2013, p. 5).

- China has become the largest financier of Africa's infrastructure, accounting for around one-third of total financing (Chen 2013; Baker & McKenzie 2015). Chinese banks have provided around US$132 billion in financing to Africa and Latin American countries since 2003 (Braütigam and Gallagher 2014; Braütigam 2016; Gallagher 2016).

- China's outward non-financial direct investment has risen from a few million dollars in the 1990s to US$118 billion in 2015 and $89 billion in the first half of 2016 (MOFCOM 2016).[16] Much of it is in economic infrastructure and manufacturing.

What Was Missing in the Previous Era? And How to Respond?

We are all beneficiaries of learning from the economic literature and international experiences in development. With the benefit of hindsight and standing on the "shoulders of giants," we examine the literature of international aid and aid effectiveness (which is newer than that on the economics of development). Such literature seems, however, to have focused on established donors' behaviors: who provides aid, donor objectives and motivations, the conditions for aid, and aid effectiveness. Very little economic work has been done on the conceptual and theoretical foundations of development finance provided by emerging economies from the "Global South."

The extensive recent literature on aid effectiveness includes Boone (1996); Burnside and Dollar (2000); Easterly et al. (2003); Easterly (2003, 2006, 2013); Collier (2007), Collier and Hoeffler (2004); Rajan and Subramanian (2008); Roodman (2007); Arndt et al. (2010); Moyo (2009); Deaton (2013); and Edwards (2014a and 2014b). One group of studies, addressing the issue of absorption and capital flight, asks, "Where did all the aid go?"[17] Only a few authors have focused on the institutional economics of aid (such as Martens et al. 2002), and more recently on the sectoral allocation of foreign aid, growth, and employment (Akramov 2012[18]; Van der Hoeven 2012[19]).

Martens et al. (2002) highlighted the "principal-agent" problems in the "donor-recipient" relationship and found that "the nature of foreign aid – with a broken information feedback loop ... put a number of inherent constraints on the performance of foreign aid programs. All these constraints are due to imperfect information flows in the aid delivery process" (p. 30). They quoted Streeten's famous question on aid with conditionality: "Why would a donor pay a recipient to do something that is anyway in his own interest? And if it is not in his own interest, why would the recipient do it anyway?" (Martens et al. 2002, p.9). Their study pointed squarely to one of the basic dilemmas in modern ODA – the nonaligned incentives between donors and recipients.[20]

Indeed, the imperfect information and the agency problem in aid with conditionality are under-researched. The role of the IMF and World Bank as "enforcers" of the global rules of development has been called into question by many authors. The IMF's Independent Evaluation Office (IEO) admits that the IMF made several mistakes during the Asian financial crisis in 1997–1998, causing unnecessary pain. "Full capital account liberalization may not be an appropriate goal for all countries at all times, and that under certain circumstances capital flow management measures can have a place in the macroeconomic policy toolkit" (IEO 2007, 2015). After the release of a staff paper on capital control (Ostry et al. 2010), Rodrik called the paper "a stunning reversal – as close as an institution can come to recanting without saying, 'Sorry, we messed up'" (Rodrik 2010).

In the face of rising international financing flows to developing countries, including Africa, we believe that some elements of the current theoretical framework may be out of date. Consider three examples.

- The IMF-World Bank debt sustainability framework (DSF) may be overly constraining for low-income countries because it does not take into account the dynamic impact of large infrastructure investment on long-term growth (Chapter 3).
- The World Bank's cost-benefit analysis on road projects has sometimes "forgotten" the important element of land price factors when considering the need for building a highway now, as opposed to 10 years later (Chapter 5).
- The World Bank's publication on "Long Term Finance,"(World Bank 2015) has missed an opportunity to summarize the experiences of East Asian countries, such as Singapore, the Republic of Korea, and China, which have successfully raised funds for long-term infrastructure financing through market instruments, state development banks, and sovereign wealth funds (Chapter 3).

And so it is high time for the IMF and the World Bank to "open up their kitchens" and welcome different development theories and ideas from the East as ingredients in their policy recommendations. Indeed, the dominant development paradigm seems to be changing: The IMF has started to rethink the "neoliberal agenda" that it had been pushing. A report by its research department points out, "instead of delivering growth, some neoliberal policies have increased inequality, in turn jeopardizing durable expansion." After capital account liberalization, "Although growth benefits are uncertain, costs in terms of increased economic volatility and crisis frequency seem more evident." (Ostry et al. 2016, p. 39). We think that democratization in development thinking is needed. Several different paradigms could coexist, and developing countries could select from the menu, based on their own developmental needs (Lin and Rosenblatt 2012).

From the angle of joint learning and concerted transformation, we argue that SSDC is more effective since these southern countries are at similar stages of structural transformation, closer together on the development path, and have similar human and institutional constraints. If they start to learn from and help each other, they would start on a more or less equal footing. They must use whatever they have and do "what they can potentially do well" – that is, develop their latent comparative advantages. Such joint learning and concerted transformation can align incentives and alleviate the principal-agent problems, the broken feedback loop, and the gaming behaviors in the aid with conditionality model (Chapters 4, 5, and 6). In Chapter 7 we discuss the new ways to overcome existing issues with South-South Development Cooperation, by using the advantage of backwardness, by targeting the sectors where an economy has latent comparative advantages,[21] and by encouraging clustering and agglomeration via establishing special economic zones or green industrial parks, to reach quick wins. Chapter 8 discusses the prospects for development finance.

***

This book should interest policymakers in government, aid agencies, academics, students, international development banks such as the World Bank Group and IMF, regional development banks (including the new banks and funds), sovereign wealth funds, public pension funds, nongovernmental organizations, civil society organizations, and private sector investors.

We hope to contribute to the debate on international aid and development cooperation, to bring fresh ideas based on experiences from countries with successful structural transformation, to deepen the understanding of alternative views from emerging market economies, to play some small part in helping establish inclusive mechanisms for aid and cooperation, and ultimately to reduce poverty and sustain development in the post-2015 era.

Notes

1. According to the OECD definition, ODA includes grants or loans that are (i) undertaken by the official sector; (ii) with promotion of economic development and welfare as the main objective; and (iii) "is concessional in character and conveys a grant element of at least 25 percent (calculated at a discount rate of 10 percent)." See www.oecd.org/dac/stats/officialdevelopmentassistancedefinitionandcoverage.htm.

2. Under the OECD-DAC definition, ODA must include grants and concessional loans to eligible recipients for the promotion of economic development and welfare from an official source (government or multilateral organization) to a set of developing countries agreed to by the Development Assistance Committee (DAC) of the OECD.

3. New Structural Economics proposes the use of neoclassical approach to study the determinants of economic structure and its evolution in the process of a country's economic development. Its main hypothesis is that the economic structure, including technology and industry as well as hard and soft infrastructure, is endogenous to endowment structure, which is given at any specific time and changeable over time. It argues that following comparative advantage (determined by the endowment structure) to develop industries is the best way to become competitive, generate economic surpluses, encourage savings, upgrade the endowment structure, and sustain industrial upgrading, income growth, and poverty reduction. It also argues that a competitive market is necessary for developing industries according to a country's comparative advantages and

a facilitating state is necessary for improving hard and soft infrastructure required for industrial upgrading (Lin 2010, 2011d).

4. That is, the country has the lowest factor costs of production in the world, but it is not competitive due to high transaction costs stemming from poor infrastructure and a weak business environment.

5. We include conventional financial instruments, medical teams, and technical assistance, but also innovative mechanisms such as preferential export buyer's credit, agricultural technology demonstration centers, and resource-financed infrastructure.

6. The emergence of new and emerging financiers of development such as China, India, and Brazil has provided low-income developing countries opportunities to select partners. By selecting different partners developing countries are actually selecting different development philosophies, sequencing and priorities. See, for example, Rodrik (2007) on development recipes; Sen (1999) and Crocker (2008) on development ethics and democracy and human rights. The sequencing and prioritization among these choices are often considered each country's internal affairs.

7. Our joint learning model is applicable only to developmental finance – the issue at hand – and not to humanitarian aid in conflicts, disasters, or epidemics.

8. Box 4.5 discusses how to measure it.

9. This is uncodified knowledge that is difficult to transfer across individuals. It is embodied in people's behavior and skills (like laying bricks or operating a machine), in institutional capacity, and in business processes.

10. See the latest World Bank Poverty Overview, using a new international poverty line: www.worldbank.org/en/topic/poverty/overview.

11. How to create a localized enabling environment for dynamic structural transformation in an economy characterized by poor infrastructure and overall distorted institutional environment was discussed in Lin 2009b, 2012b, and 2012d.

12. For overviews, see Bräutigam 2009, 2011a, 2015, 2016; Copper 2016; King 2013; Zhou et al. 2015; Dollar 2016; and Gallagher 2016.

13. See papers on this topic – including those by Summers (2014b), Krugman, Gordon, Blanchard, Koo, Eichengreen, Caballero, Glaeser, and a dozen others – at www.voxeu.org/article/secular-stagnation-facts-causes-and-cures -new-vox-ebook. Lin (2013) also discussed secular stagnation and proposed ways to get of it.

14. The "Washington Consensus" was a term coined by John Williamson (1990), originally referring to a policy package recommended for crisis-hit Latin American countries. The package of policies in the original definition included fiscal discipline, redirecting public spending from indiscriminate subsidies toward broad-based provision of pro-growth, poverty-alleviating services, broadening the tax base, interest rate liberalization, competitive exchange

rates, trade liberalization, uniform tariffs, liberalization of inward foreign direct investment, privatization of state enterprises, deregulation of market entry, prudent oversight of financial institutions, and legal protection of property rights. Subsequent to Williamson's coining, the term has been used to refer to a strongly market-based approach, labeled market fundamentalism or neoliberalism in the public discourse, although Williamson himself opposed this broader definition. We use Washington Consensus in the second, more general definition. Responding to the transition experience, Williamson proposed a much more nuanced definition, which incorporates many of the criticisms in this book (Williamson 2002).

15. See Summers 2014a.

16. According to the official statistics in the first half of 2016, "China's outward non-financial direct investment was US$88.86 billion. The complete turnover of the foreign contractual projects was US$66.05 billion and the newly-signed contractual value was US$99.69 billion; by the end of June, China has dispatched 991,000 laborers abroad." (Ministry of Commerce website, July 25, 2016; see, http://english.mofcom.gov.cn/article/newsrelease/policy releasing/201607/20160701365827.shtml).

17. See, for example, Aiyar and Ruthbah 2008; Berg et al. 2007 and 2010; and Foster and Killick 2006. The latter studies link a scaling up of aid with capital flight.

18. Akramov (2012) found that economic aid, including aid to productive sectors and economic infrastructure, contributes to economic growth by increasing domestic investment. Aid to social sectors, however, does not appear to have a significant impact on human capital and economic growth.

19. Van de Hoeven (2012) took note of China's approach of focusing on economic infrastructure and pointed to the neglect of concern for employment and inequality in the MDGs in 2000. He called for the "refocusing of development efforts," "combining a greater share of development aid for employment and productivity enhancing activities with a change in national and international economic and financial policies, so as to make employment creation (together with poverty reduction) an overarching goal" (p. 24).

20. See also Easterly 2003 and Hynes and Scott 2013.

21. An economy has a latent comparative advantage in an industry if, based on the factor costs of production determined by the economy's factor endowment structure, the industry should be competitive. However, due to high transaction costs, determined by infrastructure, logistics, and other business conditions, the industry is not yet competitive in the global market.

TWO

Structural Transformation Is Key
to Development

Box 2.1 Chapter at a glance

This chapter lays the theoretical foundation of the book by introducing the New Structural Economics (NSE) and its implications for the comparative advantage–following strategy for structural transformation.

As elaborated in the NSE, the most effective and sustainable way for job generation, poverty reduction, and inclusive development in a low-income country is to jump-start structural transformation by developing sectors in which the country has latent comparative advantages. The government could actively intervene to reduce transaction costs for these sectors by creating enclaves with good infrastructure and making the business environment attractive. A developing country adopting this approach can immediately grow dynamically and secure a virtuous circle in creating jobs and lowering poverty even though its overall infrastructure and business environment may be poor.

The chapter then discusses the importance of structural transformation for growth, job creation, and poverty reduction

Box 2.1 (*Cont.*)

in various parts of the world at different periods in history. During the Industrial Revolution, structural transformation spread in a "flying geese pattern" from Great Britain to continental Europe, the United States, and then Japan.

An analysis of the structural transformation of the Republic of Korea and China follows, showing that the process is a continuum of one wave after another and that manufacturing companies tend to relocate to countries where they have comparative advantages in relevant sectors.

Finally, it becomes clear that industrial upgrading in Brazil, China, and India is offering opportunities to other lower-income developing countries. These three are continental-sized countries, not so much leading geese but leading dragons when they start upgrading and shedding jobs, and could provide huge opportunities for sub-Saharan Africa particularly. They might create enough labor-intensive manufacturing jobs to bring sub-Saharan countries to par with most industrial countries. Even if China's manufacturing sector sheds just 10 percent of its jobs in the next few years, a pool of 8.5 million jobs might be ready to relocate abroad. The number could almost double employment in manufacturing in African countries in a few years, facilitating their inclusive structural transformation and poverty reduction.

Development Economics 3.0

Developing countries have for decades been trying to catch up with industrialized high-income countries. In the 1960s and 1970s, under prevailing development thinking, governments were advised to adopt import-substitution (IS) policies – intervening to overcome market failures – and to accelerate industrialization. In the post–World War II period, most developing countries were keenly aware of the role of industrialization in accelerating structural transformation and catch-up in Europe, Japan, and the United States. Keen to emulate them, developing countries adopted the prevailing "structuralist" paradigm, which advocated IS-led industrialization to found advanced industries similar to those in industrial countries.[1] Examples include heavy industries such as iron and steel, chemicals, machinery, and transport equipment in countries as diverse as Brazil, Egypt, Ghana, India, and the Republic of Korea. The postwar thinking can be labeled "development economics 1.0." Countries following this approach had some initial investment-led successes, but these were quickly followed by repeated crises and stagnation.

Development thinking then shifted to neoliberalism, as encapsulated in the Washington Consensus in the 1980s, in an attempt to overcome government failures. Reforms in governance and the business environment were intended to transfer to developing countries the idealized market institutions of industrialized high-income countries. These policy prescriptions may be termed "development economics 2.0." The results were lost decades of growth in developing countries – and many of them have even experienced deindustrialization (Lin 2013, p. xxiii; see also Chapter 3 of this work).

Entering the 21st century, and following the seminal work by North (1990), Sen (1999), and many others, many economists focused on institutions as source of long-term growth. For example, Acemoglu and colleagues found that "Economic institutions encouraging growth emerge when political institutions allocate power to groups with interest in broad-based property rights enforcement, when they create effective constraints on power-holders, and when there are relatively few rents to be captured by the power-holders" (Acemoglu et al. 2005, p. 387).

However, one emerging challenge associated with this line of research is the inability to establish a causal link between any particular institutional design feature and growth, reflecting the potential effects of extraneous factors on the efficacy of institutions. Indeed, as pointed out by Rodrik (2008), different institutions may have similar outcomes while the same institutions may give rise to different outcomes in different contexts. The difference between failure and success on the development path may therefore lie on singling out what makes institutions function effectively (Fofack 2014, p. 9).

While we agree that institutions are critical to development, as argued in Acemoglu and Robinson (2012),[2] the reality in developing countries is that they are inherently endowed with weak institutions and poor governance due to their stage of development. They also suffer the distortions arising from the adoption of prevailing but defunct development ideas for their modernization and nation building after World War II. So, should they focus on improving governance or on jump-starting economic development even though their governance is poor? The mainstream thinking in the global academic and development community advocates the first approach. We go for the second approach, because the improvement of governance takes time, while the need to create jobs cannot wait, and the same institutions copied from the West may produce different outcomes, as we have seen time and time again in the last few decades.

From vast empirical evidences, we understand that good governance is not a precondition for dynamic growth. We believe that it is crucial to jump-start growth in developing countries by creating enclaves in special economic zones that offer good business environments – and by removing binding constraints to help industries become competitive even though overall governance is poor. Similar arguments apply to infrastructure. Quick success in helping industries become competitive generates jobs, exports, tax revenues, resources, and experiences for further improvements in other parts of the country, and that is the best way to reduce poverty.

We also argue that institutions are endogenous: With rising incomes and economic freedoms, the people will push for better institutions, including political ones, and good governance.

Today's high-income countries did not have universal suffrage until recently, and their systems were as corrupt as many of today's developing countries. Once the poor countries today become better off and a large proportion of the population gets educated, their institutions will most likely be improved and possess many of the desirable characteristics existing in today's developed countries.[3]

After nearly two decades of neglect, many economists and policymakers have recently rediscovered the importance of structural transformation. In contrast to the "liberal institutional pluralism" focusing on institutions for effective public service delivery, the NSE brings attention back to such transformation and to industrial upgrading, which together should be the policy priority for many low- and middle-income countries. Based on the unique experiences of China and other dynamic East Asian economies, Justin Lin, as the World Bank's first chief economist from a developing country, proposed the NSE in 2009, with two books published in 2012 (Box 2.2).

The NSE is an application of the neoclassical approach that studies the determinants of the economic structure and the causes of its transformation in the process of economic development and transition. It emphasizes the role of the state in development – facilitating provision of hard and soft infrastructure, and identifying the country's existing and latent comparative advantages in a competitive market.

In his later Growth Identification and Facilitation (GIF) framework (Chapter 7), Lin (2012d) "concretized" his theory by proposing methods for identifying and facilitating the development of latent comparative–advantage sectors. The NSE and the GIF frameworks have attracted attention from emerging and developing countries because their policymakers appreciate the urgent need for structural transformation as an engine of growth and employment generation (Figure 2.1).

Box 2.2 The New Structural Economics: Helping explain the most successful developing countries' performance

The NSE starts with the observation that the nature of modern economic development is a process of continuous structural change in technologies, industries, and hard and soft infrastructure, which makes possible the continuous increase in labor productivity and thus per capita income in an economy. The optimal industrial structure in an economy *at a specific time* – the industrial structure that makes the economy most competitive domestically and internationally at that time – is endogenous to its comparative advantage, which in turn is determined by the economy's given endowment structure at that time.

Because the optimal industrial structure at any given time is endogenous to the existing factor endowments, a country trying to move up the ladder of technological development must first change its endowment structure. With capital accumulation, the economy's factor endowment structure evolves, pushing its industrial structure to deviate from the optimal determined by its previous level. Firms then need to upgrade their industries and technologies in order to maintain market competitiveness. If the economy follows its comparative advantage in developing its industries, these industries will have the lowest possible factor costs of production and thus be most competitive in domestic and world markets. As a result, they will gain the largest possible market share and generate potentially the largest surplus. Capital investment will also have the largest possible return. Consequently, households will have the highest savings propensity, resulting in an even faster upgrading of the country's endowment structure.

A developing country that follows its comparative advantage (in a comparative advantage–following, or CAF, strategy) to develop its industries can also gain from the benefits of backwardness in the upgrading process and grow faster than advanced

Box 2.2 (*Cont.*)

countries do. Enterprises in developing countries can benefit from the industrial and technological gap with developed countries by acquiring industrial and technological innovations that are consistent with their new comparative advantage through learning and borrowing from developed countries. In contrast, economies that try to deviate from their comparative advantage (in a comparative advantage–defying, or CAD, strategy) in their industrial upgrading are likely to perform poorly because firms in the new industries will be nonviable in an open, competitive market, requiring government subsidies and protection to survive, often through distortions and interventions in the market (Lin 2009b).

The main question then is: How to ensure that the economy grows in a manner that is consistent with its comparative advantage determined by its endowment structure? The goal of most firms everywhere is profit maximization, which is, all things being equal, a function of relative prices of factor inputs. The criteria that firms use to select their industries and technologies are typically the relative prices of capital, labor, and natural resources. Therefore, the precondition for firms to follow the comparative advantage of the economy in their choice of technologies and industries is to have a relative price system that can reflect the relative scarcity of these production factors in the endowment structure. Such a system exists only in a competitive market structure. In developing countries where this is usually not the case, governments must take steps to improve market institutions so as to create and protect effective competition in the product and factor markets.

In the process of industrial upgrading, firms need to have information about production technologies and product markets. If that information is scarce, each firm will need to invest resources to collect and analyze it. First movers that attempt to

Box 2.2 (*Cont.*)

enter a new industry may either succeed (because the industry is consistent with the country's new comparative advantage) or fail (because they have targeted the wrong industry).

In the case of success, their experience offers valuable and free information to other prospective entrants. They will not have monopoly rent because of competition from new entry. Moreover, these first movers often need to devote resources to train workers in the new business processes and techniques, but these workers may then be hired by competitors. First movers also generate demand for new activities and human capital that might not have existed otherwise. Even when first movers fail, their experience provides useful knowledge to other firms, yet they must bear the costs of failure. In other words, the social value of the first movers' investments is usually much larger than their private value, and there is an asymmetry between the first movers' gain from success and the cost of failure.

In addition, successful industrial upgrading in an economy also requires new types of financial, legal, and other "soft" (intangible) and "hard" (tangible) infrastructure to facilitate production and market transactions, and to allow the economy to reach its production-possibility frontier by reducing transaction costs. Improving the hard and soft infrastructure requires coordination beyond individual firms' decisions.

Economic development is therefore a dynamic process marked with externalities and one that requires coordination. While the market is a necessary basic mechanism for effective resource allocation at each given stage of development, governments must play a proactive, enabling role to facilitate an economy to move from one stage to another. They must intervene to allow markets to function properly, and can do so in four main ways: providing information about new industries that are consistent with the new comparative advantage determined by change in

Box 2.2 (*Cont.*)

the economy's endowment structure; coordinating investments in related industries and the required improvements in infrastructure; subsidizing activities with externalities in the process of industrial upgrading and structural change; and catalyzing the development of new industries by incubation or by attracting FDI to overcome the deficits in social capital and other intangible constraints (Lin 2012d, p. 21–23).

In sum, the NSE framework is three-pronged, with a recognition of differences in the optimal industrial structure for countries at different stages of development due to the differences in comparative advantage defined by their endowment structures; reliance on the market as the optimal resource allocation mechanism at any given stage of development; and appreciation of the facilitating role played by an enabling state in industrial upgrading and structural transformation.

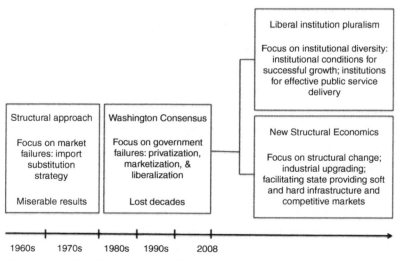

Figure 2.1 The New Structural Economics and how it relates to other approaches
Source: Fofack 2014.

Structural Transformation Is Critical to Economic Development and Poverty Reduction

History since the industrial revolution shows that the transformation from the primary activities of resource extraction and agriculture to manufacturing activities, and then to services, is crucial for productivity growth, job creation, and poverty reduction. Yet most developing countries have neglected it for too long.

Mainstream economics has for two decades paid little heed to structural transformation and industrialization. Too few resources have been invested in the economic and industrial infrastructure, causing deindustrialization in many countries. Africa, for example, has seen its share of manufacturing in GDP decline for 40 years.

In the globalized world, structural transformation is even more critical and harder to achieve because goods and services are relatively freely traded across borders, yet other factor endowments – physical, human, and natural capital (such as land) – are facing barriers to movement across borders or are completely immobile. Many developing countries have attempted to catch up with industrial countries but failed, some seemingly trapped as exporters of natural resources and primary products. In the last half a century, only 28 countries have closed the income gap with industrial countries by 10 percent or more. Among these 28, only 12 were non-European and non-resource-based countries (Lin and Rosenblat 2012).

Especially in the early stages of development, industrialization was recognized as one of the main engines of economic growth. Manufacturing, in particular, offers new and boundless possibilities for production of *tradable goods*, including technology. Manufacturing plays a crucial role in employment generation, accounting in 2013 for almost 500 million jobs worldwide, or about one-fifth of the global workforce, and allowing for greater inclusiveness and gender equality (UNIDO 2013).

Figure 2.2 shows intuitively the evidence of industrialization as an engine of growth. There is a positive and significant correlation

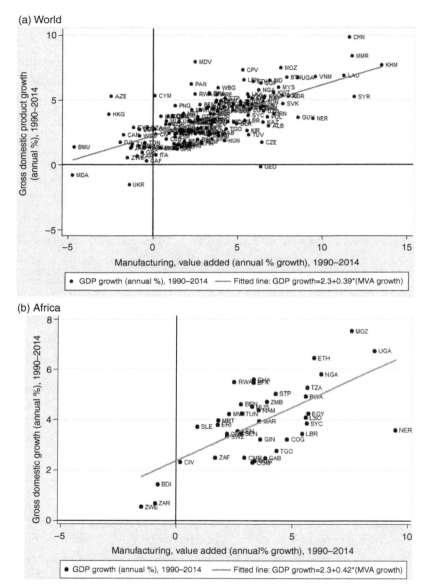

Figure 2.2 Industrialization as an engine of growth: Manufacturing value added and GDP growth rates, 1990–2014
Source: Calculated based on data from the World Bank's World Development Indicators database, accessed February 19, 2016. Updated by Yan Wang and Haixiao Wu based on Lin 2012c.

between growth of manufacturing value added (MVA) and income growth in the world and in the Africa region between 1990 and 2014. Countries with rapid MVA growth have seen their per capita GDP growth rise faster, such as Cambodia, China, Myanmar, Lao People's Democratic Republic, Vietnam, Singapore, and Malaysia. In Africa, the best performers include Uganda, Mozambique, Ethiopia, Nigeria, Tanzania, and Ghana, in that order.

Structural Transformation since the Industrial Revolution

Many countries have succeeded at structural transformation, upgrading from resource-based or agrarian economies to manufacturing power-houses. According to Angus Maddison, it took 1,400 years to double per capita income before the 18th century in Western European countries, but as the industrial revolution spread, it took only 70 years to double per capita income from the 18th century to the mid-19th century. Then it took the developed countries 35 years to double per capita income again (Maddison 2007; World Bank 2008). This process of economic transformation has been accelerated in the case of 13 rapidly growing emerging economies (mostly East Asian economies), notably the Republic of Korea; Taiwan, China; and other East Asian newly indus-trialized economies; and later, China and others, following a pattern that is well characterized by the "flying geese model" (Akamatsu 1962). The spread of industrialization in Western Europe in the 19th century, the rapid catch-up after World War II, and the East Asian miracle starting in the 1960s are all reminiscent of the flying geese pattern. In this section, we provide evidence for this assertion.

In the 1930s, economists researching catch-up growth models argued that catch-up was not random. Kuznets explored the conditions under which the industrial revolution occurred in the United Kingdom and how it spread only to those countries that had suffi-cient accumulation of capital and skilled labor, among other condi-tions (Kuznets 1930). The focus on structural transformation and industrial upgrading (Rostow 1960; Solow 1957) and cross-country catch-up (Gerschenkron 1962) can be found in Akamatsu's work on Japan (1935, 1961, and 1962), a country that started from a much lower level of income than Western European countries. In a seminal paper in the 1930s, Akamatsu documented what he called the "wild-geese flying pattern" in economic development and noted that "wild geese fly in orderly ranks forming an inverse V, just as airplanes fly in formation" (Akamatsu 1962, p. 11).

This pattern describes the sequential order of the catch-up process of industrialization of latecomer economies. It focuses on three dimensions (or stages): intra-industry; inter-industry; and international division of labor. The third element in particular involves the process of relocating industries across countries, from advanced to developing, during the latter group's process of convergence. A prominent feature of this stage is that exports of labor-intensive consumer goods start declining and capital goods begin to be exported. In this stage, a group of economies advance together through emulation and learning-by-doing.

One weakness in Akamatsu's model is, however, that he only described the flying geese pattern without linking it to a country's endowment structure and comparative advantage. He did not recognize that the market mechanism is a necessary condition for a country to follow its comparative advantage successfully. However, he noted that the accumulation of capital, technological adaptability of people, and government protection policy to promote consumer goods industries matter for the pattern (Akamatsu 1962, p. 3).

There is a fundamental difference between the traditional structuralist views and the NSE. The NSE contends that the flying geese model can be used by latecomers to catch up only if they follow the CAF approach and if the lead economy's income levels and endowment structure are not too different from theirs, allowing them to reduce their risk and cost of innovation. As long as industrialization is CAF, there is no need for the government to adopt protectionist policies because firms are viable in an open competitive market and can thus withstand market competition. Rather, the government's role is limited to facilitating firms' entry into new industries where the country has a latent comparative advantage by overcoming externalities and coordination issues inherent in the industrial upgrading and diversification process.[4]

The Spread of the Industrial Revolution: Leaders and Latecomers

The industrial revolution started in the United Kingdom in the mid-1700s, but for about 50 years did not spread to other countries because the British government forbade the export of machinery, manufacturing techniques, and skilled workers. In the 19th century it gradually spread to other countries in Western Europe. The earliest center of industrial production in continental Europe was Belgium, where production of coal, iron, textiles, glass, and armaments flourished. By 1830, French firms had employed many skilled British workers to help establish its modern textile industry, and railroads began to appear across Western Europe. The German lands were a latecomer in developing industry mainly because no centralized government existed there.

The first steam locomotive was invented in the United Kingdom in 1804, but other European countries did not start building railroads until the 1830s. The German lands, for example, produced their first locomotive in 1835, but railway construction lagged because a centralized government did not exist until 1871. After the 1840s, German coal and iron production skyrocketed, and by the 1850s, construction began on a rail network. After political unification in 1871, Germany exceeded the United Kingdom on length of new railroads, and saw rapid catch-up in the production of pig iron and other industries (Figure 2.3).

Industrialization was delayed in the United States because the country at that time lacked the basic factor endowments – labor and capital – to invest in manufacturing. When it finally picked up in the 1820s, growth was explosive. Laborers and capital came from Europe,

Length of Railways open (km)

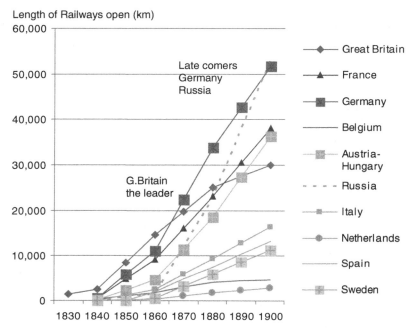

Figure 2.3 Spread of the industrial revolution: Latecomers catching up, 1800–1914

Source: Statistical Appendices, "Fontana Economic History of Europe," Vol. 4, from *Modern History Sourcebook* (Online). Available at www.fordham.edu/halsall/mod/indrevtabs1.asp.

from where political revolutions sent immigrants. The first locomotive emerged in 1826, and the first railroad in 1827. The length of the railroad surpassed that of the United Kingdom in 1850, reaching 9,021 miles, and expanded rapidly to the west in 1890 to reach 129,774 miles, longer than in continental Europe (Depew 1895, p. 111). Rapid industrialization and structural transformation then followed. In 1800, farmers made up 85 percent of the U.S. population, but 50 percent in 1860.

Gerschenkron (1962) observed that rapid industrialization could start from vastly different levels of "economic backwardness." In fact, "the more backward a country's economy, the greater was the part played by special institutional factors (government agencies, banks) designed to increase the supply of capital to the nascent industries" (Gerschenkron 1962, p. 354).

Like Akamatsu, a weakness of Gerschenkron's theory is that he did not stress that for the latecomer to be competitive, it must identify industries consistent with its comparative advantage (that is, CAF). Industrialization can start from a low level of economic development, but if that is too low, too-advanced industries will be CAD and may require heavy subsidies and protection from the state. With government support, it is possible to set up advanced industries, but for as long as they are CAD, they will be neither viable nor competitive. The government support is most likely lead to misallocation of resources and rent-seeking, resulting in slow growth and frequent crises. The advantages of backwardness may then turn into disadvantages of backwardness.[5]

Japan's Catch-Up in the Meiji Period: Learning by Importing Then Exporting

Starting with an income level that was only one-third that in the West during the 1850s, Japan achieved rapid catch-up in 50 years to become the first industrial country in Asia by around the turn of the century. After opening up trade in 1854, its government encouraged learning from Western technology and institutions by sending high-level missions, including about half of its government ministers, to the United States and Europe for nearly two years (Shimposha 2000, p. 48). After signing the Ansei Treaty in 1858, Japan lost control of its tariff policy, but the government provided facilitation by building the country's modern infrastructure and encouraging learning-by-doing. Telegraph services between Tokyo and Yokohama began in 1870. The first Japanese railroad connecting Yokohama and Shinbashi was built in 1872, and by 1900, Japan had 3,875 miles of railroad (Ito 1992). The government also introduced foreign technology by importing modern machines and hiring thousands of foreign experts to instruct Japanese workers and managers in the late 1800s (Ozawa 2004).

Throughout the Meiji period (1868–1912), Japan's top exports were raw silk yarn, tea, and marine products, which were consistent with the economy's comparative advantage. As its cotton industry grew, its imports fell steadily, and in 1890, Japan began to export large quantities of cotton, yarn, and cloth to neighboring Asian countries (i.e. intra-sector upgrading, as in Akamatsu 1962). On the institutional side, a banking system was organized and a central bank established in 1882. "The government used gold from China as compensation for the 1894–1895 war as reserves, enabling the country to set up a well-functioning gold standard system" (Ito 1992, p. 21).

Historical experiences of the industrial revolution offer several insights. First, countries on the technological frontier can play the role of the "lead goose" as the United Kingdom did. Latecomers have the economic advantage of backwardness and under certain conditions can catch up quickly and even overtake the lead goose. Second, capital accumulation was necessary but not sufficient for success. Political stability, openness to trade, and labor mobility were also important for acquiring new technology and developing new industries. Further, governments were required to play a facilitating role for providing incentives to the first movers and coordinating requirements in hard and soft infrastructure, as in Germany, Japan, and the United States. Without the existence of a centralized state in Germany since 1871, there would have been no railroad or industrial revolution.

More important, selecting the right target country is critical for catching up. Some European countries could catch up with the United Kingdom relatively quickly because their stages of development were not too far from the leader (Table 2.1). According to Maddison (2001), per capita incomes of France, Germany, and the United States were about 60–75 percent of the United Kingdom's in 1870.[6] During the Meiji restoration, Japan targeted the industries of Prussia (later, Germany), and its per capita income was about 40 percent of the latter. Thus it was realistic for Japan to target Germany

TABLE 2.1 *Catch-up prewar and postwar*

	Europe targeted the United Kingdom, gaps were small		Japan targeted Germany during the Meiji Restoration			Japan targeted the United States after WWII		
	1870	% of the United Kingdom	1890	1900	% of Germany	1950	1960	% of the United States
France	1,876	59	2,376	2,876		5,186	7,398	
Germany	1,839	58	2,428	2,985	100	3,881	7,705	
United Kingdom	3,190	100	4,009	4,492		6,939	8,645	
United States	2,445	77	3,392	4,091		9,561	11,328	100
Japan	737		1,012	1,180	40	1,921	3,986	35

	Asian NIEs (4 tigers) incl. the Republic of Korea targeted Japan in the 1960s–1980s			China targeted East Asian NIEs incl. the Republic of Korea			Latecomers started to target China after 2000		
	1960	1970	% of Japan	1980	1990	% of the Republic of Korea	2000	2008	% of PRC
United Kingdom	8,645	10,767		12,931	16,430		20,353	23,742	
United States	11,328	15,030		18,577	23,201		28,467	31,178	
Japan	3,986	9,714	**100**	13,428	18,789		20,738	22,816	
Korea, Rep. of	1,226	2,167	**25**	4,114	8,704	**100**	14,375	19,614	
China	662	778		1,061	1,871	**23**	3,421	6,725	**100**
India	753	868		938	1,309		1,892	2,975	**44**
Vietnam	799	735		757	1,025		1,809	2,970	**44**

Note: Targeted countries are underlined, following countries in bold.
Source: Authors' calculations based on the Angus Maddison database.

rather than the United Kingdom or the United States, which were too far ahead on development. Even though many nation states tried to catch up, Japan succeeded and became the first industrialized nation from the East because it chose the right country to target.

Post–World War II: The United States Showing the Way to Japan and Others

The economies of Western Europe and Japan have enjoyed unprecedented growth and technological upgrading in the decades since World War II in the so-called golden age of capitalism (1950–1974). During the period, nearly all developing countries pursued *dirigiste* capitalism but, save for Japan, the Republic of Korea and other East Asian tigers, did not succeed. Why?

The NSE contends that the crux of Japan's and East Asia's success was that their development followed closely their comparative advantage (CAF) and their governments played the facilitator's role (Lin 2010; Lin and Monga 2012).

Just before World War II, textiles and other light industrial goods accounted for 60–75 percent of all Japanese exports, and Japan's textile industry was at its peak (Ito 1992, p. 24). In the 1960s, when its per capita GDP was about 40 percent that of the United States and it had established a strong industrial base, Japan targeted U.S. industries. Japan's historical labor statistics record that a rising share of labor in its manufacturing sector coincided with a declining share of labor in that in the United States. In the 1960s–1970s, Japan supported its heavy manufacturing sector, including machinery and automobiles. In the 1980s–1990s, just as the United States was upgrading its industrial base, Japan expanded its shares in the home appliance, electronics, and computer markets (Figure 2.4).

Figure 2.5 shows the employment shares in the United States during 1958–2005 for five subsectors selected from 99 manufacturing industries, from most labor intensive to most capital intensive.

% of employment by sector

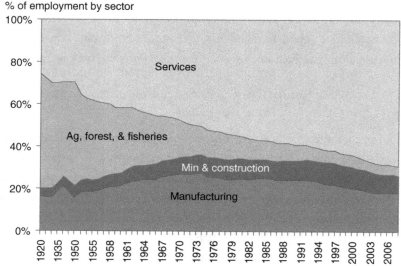

Figure 2.4 Structural transformation in Japan – manufacturing increase
followed by slow decline as services expanded (percent)
Note: Figures refer to shares of employment by sector.
Source: Authors based on Historical Statistics of Japan (On-line). Available
at: www.stat.go.jp/english/data/chouki/index.htm.

As the capital–labor ratio increased over time, industrial and
employment structures changed dramatically. Specifically, the
share of labor employed in the most labor-intensive sectors such as
fabrics declined monotonically. In sectors such as computer manufacturing, the share of labor employed first increased and then
declined, showing a hump or inverse V-shape. In industries such as
aircraft and automobile manufacturing, which are capital intensive
but subject to labor-saving scale economies, the share of labor
showed a slow and declining trend. In the most technology-
intensive sectors such as plastics, including fiber optics and lenses,
the share of employment showed a monotonic increase, indicating
that the United States still maintains a comparative advantage in
these industries. In general, the manufacturing sectors started to

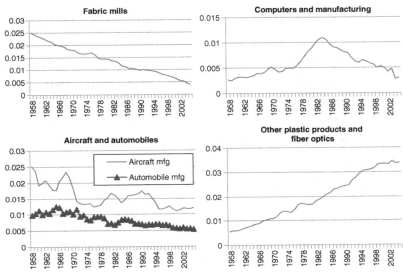

Figure 2.5 The United States as leader of transformation, shares in total employment for selected subsectors, 1958–2005

Notes: The subsectors, selected from the 99 industrial sectors, are ranked by their capital–labor ratio. These are the: (i) labor-intensive sector (industry 313210, broadwoven fabric mills); (ii) mid-level capital–labor intensity (industry 334111, electronic computer manufacturing); (iii) high capital intensity (industry 336411, aircraft and industry 336111, automobile); and (iv) high technical intensity (industry 326199, other plastic products manufacturing including fiber lens, windshield, and optics). The 1997, 6-digit NAICS codes (473 industries) were used.

Source: Ju et al. 2011. Based on NBER-CES manufacturing industry data for 1958–2005.

shed labor in the 1970s, while the services sector created more jobs throughout the period. This process accelerated in the 1990s.

Why has the employment structure in the United States changed so rapidly? First, simultaneous improvements in education, financial, and legal institutions as well as in hard infrastructure has allowed firms to constantly innovate and create new industries and exhaust the set of production possibilities (Harrison and Rodriguez-Clare 2010). Second, this process has been accelerated by globalization. Because the United

States maintained an open trade regime and a liberal investment policy, industrial transformation that started in the 1970s–1980s exceeded that of other countries (McMillian and Rodrik 2011). Third, the behavior of multinational corporations has been important. Using firm-level data related to outward FDI from the Ministry of International Trade and Industry (MITI) of Japan and from the United States, Lipsey et al. (2000) found that U.S. firms appeared to reduce employment at home by allocating labor-intensive parts of their production to affiliates in developing countries.

And why was economic growth in Japan not sustained after the 1970s? From the mid-1950s to 1973, Japan was able to sustain rapid growth for nearly 20 years. But in 1973 that growth started declining for three reasons: oil crises, a decline in investment, and a slowdown in technological progress. "Japan finally caught up with the U.S. and the Western European countries technologically in the mid-1970s . . . [and] since it was harder to develop a country's own new technology compared to merely obtaining a license, Japan's growth rate then had to fall" (Ito 1992, p. 72). In other words, Japan's advantage of backwardness had been exhausted. The economy was then constrained mainly by the speed of indigenous innovations on the global technology frontier. Japan had to relocate some of its production base to the Republic of Korea; Taiwan, China; and other NIEs because of rising domestic labor costs due to the loss of its comparative advantage in labor-intensive sectors.

Transformation in a "Flying Geese Pattern" in East Asia

It has been well-documented that several generations of lead geese played significant roles in the rapid development of the East Asian economies. From 1965 to 1990, Japan emerged as the world's biggest exporter of manufactured goods, increasing its share of the world market from about 8 percent to almost 12 percent. Its success was followed by a second generation of economies in the 1970s

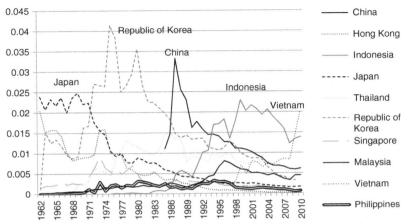

Figure 2.6 Share of textile sector export in total merchandise exports share of textile exports: five generations of flying geese (Japan, the Republic of Korea, China, Indonesia, and Vietnam)
Note: Figures based on SITC rev 1, 3–4 digits.
Source: Authors, based on UN Comtrade data via WITS.

(Hong Kong, China; the Republic of Korea; Singapore; and Taiwan, China), a third generation in the 1980s (Indonesia, Malaysia, the Philippines, and Thailand, or ASEAN4), and a fourth generation in the 1990s (China and Vietnam) (Gill and Kharas 2007, p. 81).

What is less well-studied, however, is how this flying geese pattern evolved at the subsector level, how the "jumping" of an industry from one country to another took place, and how the Republic of Korea ceded its dominance in labor-intensive subsectors to the third generation of geese – ASEAN4, China, and Vietnam. Using United Nations Comtrade data, we show graphically (Figure 2.6) that:

- There is an inverse U-shape in some subsectors where the lead goose loses comparative advantage to its followers (as in Akamatsu 1962). Since Akamatsu's transformation cycle could last for over 100 years, the inverse U-shape emerges only when simple measures such as shares of exports in the sector are used to illustrate the pattern. Each specific sector may have several generations of countries playing the role of lead goose sequentially in different periods as each country's endowment structure changes.

- In textiles – an upstream but labor-intensive industry – five generations emerged sequentially. Japan ceded to the Republic of Korea in the 1980s, after which China emerged in the 1990s, though its textile exports are now losing steam as labor costs rise and the employment share declines. ASEAN4, particularly Indonesia and Vietnam, and countries that can expand market share rapidly would have a better chance to benefit by following China.

- In the 1970s, Japan lost its leading position in the apparel and clothing sector to the Republic of Korea, whose clothing exports show a clear hump shape as it ceded its leading position to China in 1989. China emerged later than ASEAN4, but its low wages and efficient industrial clusters in many provinces enabled it to gain dominance. After many years in the dominant position, China is now losing its comparative advantage due to rising wages and will gradually cede its market shares to ASEAN4, Vietnam, and countries that can seize the opportunity to rapidly expand exports.

A key point from this analysis is that China's graduation from these labor-intensive industries offers huge opportunities to other low-income countries.

The Republic of Korea: An Example of Successful Industrial Upgrading[7]

The industrial upgrading of the Republic of Korea since 1962 is often described as a good example of flying geese catch-up.[8] The share of manufactures in GDP rose from a mere 9 percent in 1953 to 30.1 percent in 1988, while that of agriculture and mining shrunk to single digits in the 1990s.

During this phase of industrial upgrading – guided by export-oriented industrialization – the benefits of economic backwardness were exploited with sequential structural transformation from labor-intensive industries to capital-intensive industries. Until the early 1980s, labor-intensive products, primarily wood manufactures and clothing, had a combined share of about 60 percent and accounted for the majority of total exports. Since 1983, capital-intensive machinery and transport equipment products have accounted for the majority of exports; after the mid-1990s, their share exceeded half of total exports.

We argue that the Republic of Korea's success was due in part to its adherence to its comparative advantage, which evolved over time with changes in its factor endowments, suggesting flying geese catch-up patterns[9] (Figure 2.7a shows the intra- and inter-industrial dimension). The country moved up the value chain from exports of clothing to exports of textiles and to production of synthetic fibers

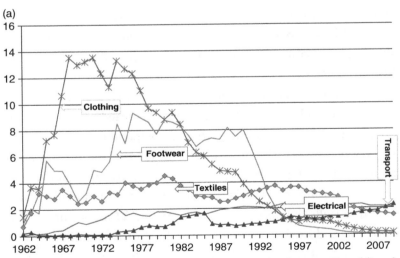

Figure 2.7a Revealed comparative advantage of industries, Republic of Korea

RCA = share of an industry in the economy's exports/its share in global exports.

Note: Based on SITC rev 1, 2 digits.

Source: UN Comtrade data via WITS, authors' calculations.

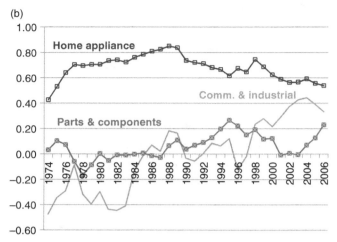

Figure 2.7b Trade specialization index of electronics, Republic of Korea
Note: Trade specialization index = (export – import)/(export + import) for
each industry.
Source: Korea Electronic Association.

(Lim 2011). In the electronics industry, a comparative advantage
recorded by the net trade index reveals industrial upgrading from
simple goods to more sophisticated goods (Lin and Chang 2009).
Starting with the assembly of radios from imported components, the
economy obtained a comparative advantage in the home appliance
industry (World Bank 1987). The country started to gain comparative advantage in electronic parts and components (transistors and
semiconductors) in the mid-1980s, and later in information, communication, and industrial electronics in the 1990s (Figure 2.7b).

Along the inter-industrial dimension, the economy maintained
a high revealed comparative advantage (RCA) in clothing exports
until the end of the 1960s, followed by footwear until the 1980s.
In the 1990s, it rapidly developed a high RCA in electronics exports,
which was more recently replaced by transport equipment exports.

The Republic of Korea's flying geese catch-up also had an
international dimension involving the relocation of an industry

from one country to another. For example, it gained a sharp increase in RCA in footwear in the mid-1960s partly as a result of manufacturing alliances and technology cooperation between local and Japanese firms prompted by increasing wages in Japan, which had been weakening the latter's competitiveness in the sector. A steep decrease in its RCA in the mid-1990s indicates that higher wages in the Republic of Korea had led to a relocation of factories to China, Indonesia, and Vietnam (The Committee for the Sixty-Year History of the Korean Economy 2010). Since the end of the 1980s, when a liberal policy was adopted, outward foreign investment from the Republic of Korea's labor-intensive industries has increased, with its main destination being Asian countries.

China's Structural Transformation: Learning and Industrial Upgrading

China's success over the past three decades is based on two pillars. First is adopting a dual-track approach to reforms, giving transitory protection to capital-intensive sectors, and liberalizing entry to labor-intensive sectors, thereby following its comparative advantage to achieve stability and dynamic transformation simultaneously. Second is as a latecomer, choosing an economic development strategy that tapped into the potential advantage of backwardness along the lines of the flying geese pattern.

Industrial development in China after reforms launched in 1979 has essentially followed the country's comparative advantage (it is CAF). When China started its economic transformation, it was an agrarian economy with agriculture as its largest sector, accounting for 79 percent of employment. Per capita income was US$154 in 1978, less than one-third of the average of sub-Saharan African countries. Like many of those countries today, China was an exporter of primary products: As late as 1984, half of China's exports were

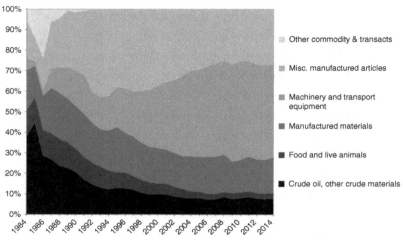

Figure 2.8 China's export structure: From raw materials in the 1980s to labor-intensive manufacturing products in the mid-1990s
Note: Manufactured material includes iron and steel, refined gasoline, chemicals, and so on.
Source: Lin and Wang 2008, updated by Yan Wang using Comtrade data.

in raw materials including oil, coal, food and animals, and other agricultural products (Figure 2.8).

The first industrial upgrade from resources to labor-intensive products happened in 1986, when exports of textiles and clothing exceeded crude oil. The second upgrade came in 1995, when Chinese exports of machinery and electronics exceeded textiles and clothing, showing that China has started the transition from exporting traditional labor-intensive exports to nontraditional labor-intensive processes (assembly lines). The third occurred after 2001 following China's accession to the World Trade Organization, locking in liberalization of trade in goods and services and making Chinese laws and regulations conform to international standards. Regulatory reforms led to rapidly rising FDI inflows, bringing in new technologies and processes and raising the level of product sophistication.[10]

The evolution of China's export structure in the last three decades reflects significant structural transformation in the flying geese style that has enabled the country to graduate from exporting labor-intensive products such as apparel, textiles, and leather to producing more sophisticated items such as home appliances, office machines, and electric machinery.[11] Unlike the case of the Republic of Korea, FDI played a critical role in China's industrial upgrading. More specifically,

- Inward FDI helped industrial upgrading. Many studies have pointed out that foreign investors are quick to identify a country's comparative advantage and serve as the most dynamic forces in industrial development and upgrading (Harrison and Rodríguez-Clare 2010; Aghion et al. 2011). In our view, foreign investors serve as identifiers of growth sectors, providing advanced technology and helping reduce first-mover risks and transaction costs when firms attempt to enter a new product or market. China's capital–labor ratio in manufacturing increased from 0.4 in 1985 to nearly 4.0 in 2007, when foreign-invested enterprises accounted for about 20 percent of tax revenue, 55 percent of imports and exports, and over 80 percent of high-tech exports (MOFCOM 2013).
- In the last decade, FDI inflows have been shifting toward higher value-added products, parts and components, and services. Investors from Taiwan, China, have provided much-needed managerial skills and technology that firms need in electronics and information technology. These firms are moving their manufacturing of electronic parts and components to China. Wholesale and retailing have shown the fastest growth rate in recent years, as China has moved to promoting domestic consumption. The services sector accounted for over 51 percent of GDP in 2015.
- The process of three-stage upgrading shows the importance of learning-by-exporting from lower-end manufacturing goods to higher-value-added goods and subsequently to services. Initial learning activities occurred within sectors, then gradually spilled

over horizontally to new sectors (and eventually diversified through outward FDI to other countries) (Lin and Wang 2008).

The Emergence of Leading Dragons

China is at a stage where Western countries and Japan were in the 1960s and where other Asian economies (Hong Kong, China; the Republic of Korea; Singapore; and Taiwan, China) found themselves in during the 1980s. As labor-intensive industries matured, wages increased, and firms moved into more technologically sophisticated industries in accordance with the upgrading of the underlying endowment structure. In Western countries and the Asian tigers, as the capital intensity of production in manufacturing increased, there was an overall contraction in manufacturing jobs and a reallocation of resources toward services. For example, the share of manufacturing employment in the United States fell from 17 percent in the 1980s to 9 percent in 2004, and in Japan from 18 percent to 12 percent in the same period. When labor-intensive industries in the high-wage countries shut, their jobs relocated to other lower-wage economies, such as the East Asian tigers.

China's labor costs are rising rapidly, while the structure of its industries, exports, and employment is changing. Many Chinese economists argue that the country has already absorbed its surplus labor and approached the Lewis turning point (Cai et al. 2009; Huang and Jiang 2010). Recent data indicate that China's manufacturing wages grew fast, from just over US$150 a month in 2005 to around US$350 in 2010 and to US$500 in 2013 (Figure 2.9).[12] More precisely, the wage gap between China and other upper middle-income countries is closing, a trend that will likely continue with certainty over the coming decade.

China's thirteenth Five-Year Plan projects that over the years 2016–2020, the economy will average at least 6.5 percent a year

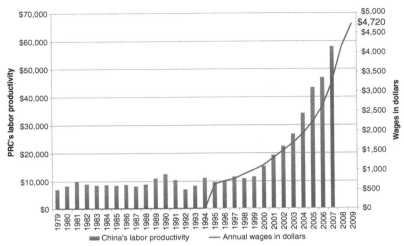

Figure 2.9 Labor productivity and average wages in China's manufacturing
Sources: Dinh et al. 2012 and updated based on National Bureau of
Statistics of China. 2010. *China Statistical Yearbook*. Beijing.

growth. It also proposes that real wages will grow as fast as GDP, and
real per capita income will double relative to 2010. Both growth rates
are likely to be achieved. When combined with continued currency
appreciation, China's real wages could approach US$1,000 per month
within five years, or about the level of some of the higher middle-
income countries today (like Brazil or Turkey) and US$2,000 per
month by 2030 (as in the Republic of Korea or Taiwan, China).

Due to an enormous population size of 1.3 billion, when China
loses comparative advantages and starts to shed labor-intensive
industries, it will be a leading dragon instead of a leading goose,
offering opportunities to a much large numbers of developing countries. Spillovers from the leading dragon phenomenon spurred by
rising Chinese wages are already helping relocate its labor-intensive
jobs to other lower-wage countries. Many such countries in China's
neighborhood, including Cambodia, the Lao People's Democratic
Republic, Vietnam, and even Bangladesh, are emerging as new
growth nodes for garment, footwear, and other labor-intensive

industries. The number of jobs that each country can attract depends on the incentives and facilitating package it offers to investors.

Developing countries, especially labor-abundant ones, can benefit by attracting labor-intensive enterprises relocating out of China. In particular, in Southeast Asia, the scarcity of local entrepreneurial skills and investment capital are invariably the top two constraints for competitive manufacturing. Self-evidently, the availability of inward FDI enables them to overcome these constraints and take advantage of enterprises relocating from China and other emerging markets. Figure 2.10 shows that China leads Brazil, Russia, India, Korea, and South Africa in outward FDI, which climbed from a few million dollars to more than US$116 billion in 2014 (UNCTAD Statistics 2015). A large proportion of outward FDI has been invested in neighboring Asian countries, mostly in green field investments.

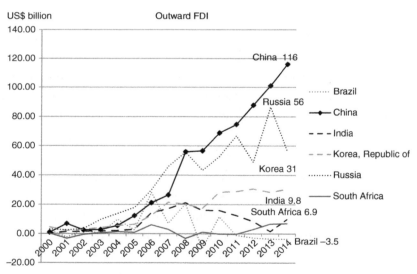

Figure 2.10 Outward FDI from China and other countries, 1995–2014
Note: According to Chinese government statistics, China's outward FDI was US$118 billion in 2015 and $89 billion in the first half of 2016 (MOFCOM 2016).
Source: Authors' calculations based on UNCTAD data, accessed November 2015.

*In Sum, Industrial Upgrading in BRICS Countries Provides
Opportunities to Low-Wage Countries*

Due to the sheer size of China's labor market, the number of jobs its industrialization will create for low-income countries is potentially huge. As employment statistics for manufacturing are extremely sparse and tentative, we cannot provide exact estimates of potential job relocation and use rough calculations. In 2014, China employed about 124 million workers nationwide in manufacturing, a majority in labor-intensive sectors (about 85 million). Rising wages will force China to upgrade to higher value-added and more capital-intensive and technology-intensive sectors, and to relocate jobs to countries with lower wages. India currently employs about 9 million workers, and Brazil about 13 million. These emerging market countries employ about 110 million workers whose jobs could potentially be relocated to other developing countries in the coming decades.

China, Brazil, and India are continent-sized countries. They are not leading geese but leading dragons when they start upgrading and shed jobs, and they could provide huge opportunities for developing countries, including those in sub-Saharan Africa. Even if China's manufacturing sector sheds 10 percent of its total employment in the next few years, a pool of 8.5 million jobs could be ready to relocate overseas, almost doubling manufacturing employment in sub-Saharan Africa in a few years and jump-starting industrialization more effectively than international aid has ever done.

Notes

1. See, for example, Prebisch 1950.
2. We agree with Acemoglu and Robinson's views that inclusive institutions matter. However, we disagree with them about the root of distortions and political captures in Latin America and many developing countries. They failed to recognize that many Latin American countries were prosperous before the 20th century, and many distortive institutions that favored industrial elites did not exist until the 1930s, when the political system in Latin America was dominated by the

landed class. The "extractive" institutions were adopted not because of the lobby of vested industrialists (because they did not exist at that time) but because of the adoption of comparative-advantage-defying, import substitution strategy for the sake of national building by the landed class (see Lin 2009).

3. There is a heated debate on the linkage between development, governance, and democracy. See, for example, Carothers and De Gramont (2013); Crocker (2008); and Bell (2015). This however is beyond the scope of this book.

4. An industry is an economy's latent comparative advantage if, based on the factor costs of production which are determined by the economy's endowment structure, the economy can be competitive in this industry. However, due to high transaction costs (which are determined by infrastructure, logistics, and other business conditions), the economy may not yet be competitive in the global market in this industry.

5. See detailed discussion in Lin 2016.

6. The United Kingdom's per capita income in 1870 was 3,190 in 1990 international Geary-Khamis dollars, and that of most Western European countries was 1,500–2,500 such dollars.

7. The authors thank Kwang Park for this section on Korea.

8. The Republic of Korea's industrial upgrading process between the 1960s and the 1980s can be roughly divided into three phases: (i) the "takeoff" phase (1962–1973); (ii) the Heavy and Chemical Industry (HCI) drive phase (1973–1979); and (iii) the liberalization phase (1980–later) (World Bank 1987). For details of industrial policies, see World Bank 1987; Krueger 1997; Suh 2007; and Lim 2011.

9. Some critics have argued that the Republic of Korea adopted a CAD strategy; see Lin and Chang 2009. We consider its policies as consistent with the NSE and the GIF framework.

10. There is, however, a myth on the level of export sophistication, discussed at length in Koopman et al. (2008) and Lin and Wang (2008). In fact, over half of exports by value added were foreign value-added, i.e. goods and services produced by foreign-invested enterprises. Among high-technology goods, over 80 percent were exported by such enterprises.

11. In the context of vertical disintegration of supply chains, the flying geese pattern still exists as multinationals move the labor-intensive part of their production (often, assembly) to China and other low-wage countries, keeping the critical components and parts at home. This does not change our fundamental premise. As wages increase in China, labor-intensive assembly lines will shift to other lower-income countries, and China will upgrade to higher value-added components and parts, as well as higher-tech products.

12. From *Oxford Analytica*, March 28, 2011. During 2010–2011, China's minimum wage in 30 municipalities rose by at least 25 percent.

THREE

Traditional Aid Is Ineffective for Structural Transformation

Box 3.1 Chapter at a glance

Reviewing recent debates and the lack of consensus on international aid's effectiveness, this chapter underlines the need for new ideas and practices. With no single, generally accepted definition of aid and its effectiveness, we provide one from the angle of structural transformation.

Economic development is a process of continuous structural changes in technologies, with industries increasing labor productivity, and hard and soft infrastructure reducing transaction costs. Traditional development aid would be effective in reducing poverty and in achieving inclusive and sustainable development if it were used for augmenting the resources under the command of governments in low-income countries and for releasing the bottlenecks of structural transformation, such as improving infrastructure in special economic zones and building roads to ports. In this way, it could jump-start dynamic structural transformation by facilitating growth in sectors of latent comparative advantage.

Where real progress has been made, we see a departure from the Washington Consensus or market fundamentalism. So it is time for Washington-based international institutions to "open their kitchens" and incorporate new ideas from the East.

The Recent Debate on International Aid and Its Effectiveness

The effectiveness of international aid has been one of the most complex and contentious issues in development economics in recent years, and the debate has heated up more recently. According to the Organisation for Economic Co-operation and Development (OECD), official development assistance (ODA) includes grants and concessional loans to eligible recipients for the promotion of economic development and welfare from an official source (a government or multilateral organization) to a set of developing countries agreed to by the Development Assistance Committee (DAC) of the OECD (Development Initiatives 2013, p. 317).

Since the 1960s, over US$2 trillion has been provided as ODA, including bilateral and multilateral aid and a portion of non-transferred aid (Figure 3.1), but its effectiveness is still hotly contested.[1] A basic consensus on its effect on economic development is lacking, despite a plethora of empirical studies subsequent to influential studies by Boone (1996) and Burnside and Dollar (2000).

One group of scholars believes that ODA is ineffective because, all too often, individuals in the South are seen "primarily as passive

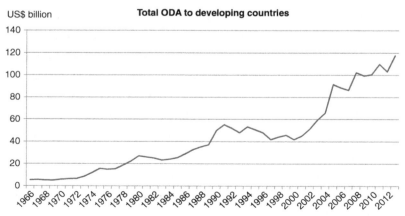

Figure 3.1 Total ODA to developing countries, 1966–2013
Source: Authors based on the World Bank AidFlow data, accessed October 30, 2015.

recipients of the benefits of cunning development programs" (Sen 1999, p. 11).[2] It is ineffective because it creates dependency, fosters corruption, encourages currency overvaluation, and crowds out private investment (Easterly 2003, 2006; 2013; Easterly et al. 2004; Moyo 2009). In the other camp, Sachs (2009) and Stiglitz (2002) believe that aid volumes have been too low and that large increases could really help reduce poverty. They advocate a major rethinking of how international aid is provided.

Empirical studies, with different results, have formed no consensus. Rajan and Subramanian (2008) found that aid had no significant impact on growth, while Arndt et al. (2010) reached the opposite conclusion: "Aid has a positive and statistically significant causal effect on growth over the long run" (p. 1).

Angus Deaton argues in his 2013 book, *The Great Escape*, that there is no easy answer, although he later considers that foreign aid "has made things worse, particularly in terms of health care. But foreign aid also undermines the development of local state capacity." This is most obvious in countries – mostly in Africa – where the government receives aid directly and aid flows are large relative to fiscal expenditure (often more than half the total). Deaton goes on: "Such governments are not accountable to anyone, except to donors. Donor agencies need to disburse money just as much as poor-country governments need to receive it, if not more so." So he suggests a ceiling of foreign aid as a proportion of fiscal revenue, since beyond that, aid would be ineffective (Deaton 2013b, p. 3).

A paper by Galiani et al. (2015) found that the effect of aid on growth is positive and significant and that the main channel for aid to promote growth is by *increasing physical investment*. This result is consistent with that of Akramov (2012), who found that economic aid, including aid to productive sectors and economic infrastructure, contributes to economic growth by increasing domestic investment. Aid to social sectors, however, does not appear to have a significant impact on human capital and economic growth.

Sebastian Edwards wrote a comprehensive paper that reviews the effectiveness of international aid from a historical perspective and shows that it is a relatively new concept in economics generally and is heavily influenced by evolving new thinking in the subfield of development economics. He emphasizes the role of "ownership" of aid programs by recipient countries as a way of increasing effectiveness, arguing that

> there is little hope of making significant progress in these debates if the economics profession continues to rely heavily on cross-section and panel regressions. In order to move forward and find out under what conditions aid is helpful and when it fails, these works need to be supplemented by in depth case studies that follow a country's history for many decades, focus on specific details of policy, understand the way in which the authorities relate to aid officials, concentrate on the political economy of reforms, and scrutinize the beliefs of politicians, policymakers, and other key players. Only then will the profession be able to understand the intricacies of foreign assistance and its level of effectiveness. (Edwards 2014a, p. 2–3)

We agree with this assessment.

Our book focuses on structural transformation and its financing mechanism – going beyond aid and aid effectiveness. From the angle of structural transformation, and based on the New Structural Economics (NSE), we divide the recent history of aid and South-South Development Cooperation (SSDC) – which combines aid, trade, and investment to achieve broader development goals – into five periods.

1950–1970s: Failed Structural Transformation for Most Countries. "Development economics 1.0" and import-substitution policies prevailed, when countries engaged in comparative advantage–defying (CAD) strategies advocated by structuralism (Box 2.2).[3] Donors from the North and South supported large capital-intensive projects, huge farms, and enormous infrastructure projects, but the capital-intensive firms were not viable because they failed to follow their comparative advantages. Many developing countries suffered debt crises.

1980–1990s: Structural Transformation at Work for Some, a Lost Decade for Others. This period saw great divergence, and different development strategies were adopted in East Asia and Africa. In East Asia, developing countries learned from East Asia's newly industrialized economies, which followed a CAF strategy and developed labor-intensive industries. A supportive development partnership was established between donors and recipients in the region, with countries in full control of their reform agendas. Many African countries struggled with structural adjustment loans, ignoring structural transformation, and were forced to open their capital accounts, resulting in a lost decade. After 1991, Russia and former Soviet Union countries suffered from shock therapy imposed by proponents of the Washington Consensus and lost much of their national wealth. Meanwhile at the World Bank, a comprehensive development framework focusing on poverty reduction was promoted in 1999 in order to achieve Millennium Development Goals (MDGs). An agenda to improve the quality of growth, i.e. an inclusive and sustainable development with good governance was implemented.[4]

2000–2008: New Momentum in South-South Development Cooperation. The first Forum of China-Africa Cooperation was held in Beijing in 2000, with 42 African leaders attending. China, India, and other emerging market economies had become increasingly more important trading partners and providers of aid and investment to other developing countries, though many of their projects were not up to international standards, opening themselves to criticism. During the Global Conference on Scaling Up Poverty Reduction in Shanghai in 2004, World Bank President James Wolfensohn announced that "the Washington Consensus is dead." The global development community started to heed the miraculous growth and poverty reduction in China and other East Asian economies.

2008–2014: Looking East for Answers. With the global financial crisis and the sluggish recovery, BRICS countries become the main engine of global growth. With the weakness in the economic recovery in the West, developing countries' policymakers started looking East. Justin Lin (one of this book's authors) was appointed Chief Economist of the World Bank, showing the worldwide interest in ideas from China. Mainstream economics and market fundamentalism still prevailed, however, in Washington-based international financial organizations. South-South cooperation climbed quickly, from a few million dollars to many billions. The NSE proposed by Lin started to take root in African countries, although the response from Washington-based institutions was lukewarm. Many special economic zones (SEZs) and industrial parks had emerged and attracted labor-intensive industries from China and India to low-wage developing countries.

2015–Present: The "New Multilateralism." The BRICS established the New Development Bank, and 57 member countries founded the Asian Infrastructure Investment Bank (AIIB), at the dawn of the new multilateralism – the age of South-led multilateralism. For recipient countries the age of choices has begun with multiple development partners from the North and South, but theories underlying SSDC are still not clear, requiring a re-analysis of what is missing in development theory and practice.

What Kind of Development Partnership Has Worked, and What Has Not?

The rest of this chapter draws heavily on the two authors' discussions with African policymakers and donor country officials.[5] Since 1960, nearly US$1 trillion of ODA has been provided to sub-Saharan Africa by OECD Development Assistance Committee (DAC) countries (Figure 3.2). But has it been effective?[6]

No, according to Angus Deaton, among others. He shows that in sub-Saharan Africa, "when aid fell off, after the end of the Cold War, growth picked up; the end of the Cold War took away one of the main rationales for aid to Africa, and African growth rebounded" (Deaton 2013, p. 285).

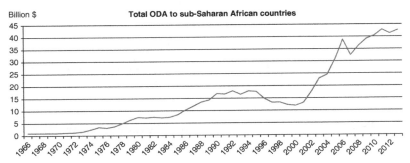

Figure 3.2 Total ODA to sub-Saharan Africa, 1966–2013
Sources: Authors based on the World Bank AidFlow data. The total includes bilateral and multilateral aid with some proportion not-transferred, accessed November 1, 2015.

Many donors still cling to the hydraulic idea that aid provides capital to poor countries that cannot otherwise afford it and thus gives them a better future. But this is contradicted by the data, because aid does not work like investment, and indeed the whole idea makes no sense given the access that many poor countries have to private international capital markets (Deaton 2013 p. 289).

We fully agree with him that aid as currently defined is less effective than South-South Development Cooperation, which combines trade, aid, and investment.

Therefore, in the following sections, we too argue that traditional aid is not effective, for the following reasons:

- Traditional aid is neither effective nor sufficient in helping developing countries to address their growth bottlenecks, because the mainstream economics has neglected structural transformation. Power generation is an example.
- The Washington Consensus and Washington–based institutions made many mistakes on advising on capital account liberalization.
- Mainstream economics may have been overly constraining in the IMF–World Bank Debt Sustainability Framework, which needs to be improved.

- Aid with conditionality is not conducive to country ownership for development.
- China as a recipient country presents a good country-ownership model where real partnership has worked, marking a departure from Washington Consensus prescriptions.

Traditional Aid Is Insufficient to Alleviate Infrastructure Bottlenecks

Infrastructure has long been recognized as the basic public good that governments should try to provide. Adam Smith outlined the "proper expenses of the sovereign" in *The Wealth of Nations, Book V, Ch. I,* including "to enforce contracts and provide justice system, grant patents and copy rights, provide public goods such as infrastructure, provide national defense and regulate banking." It was the role of the government to provide goods "of such a nature that the profit could never repay the expense to any individual" such as roads, bridges, canals, and harbors (p. 211). He also encouraged invention and new ideas through patent enforcement and support of infant industry monopolies. He supported partial public subsidies for elementary education, and he believed that competition among religious institutions would provide a general benefit to society. In such cases, however, Smith argued for local rather than centralized control: "Even those public works which are of such a nature that they cannot afford any revenue for maintaining themselves . . . are always better maintained by a local or provincial revenue, under the management of a local and provincial administration, than by the general revenue of the state" (*Wealth of Nations,* V.i.d.18, p. 689).

Over two centuries later, large infrastructure gaps in the developing world are the biggest obstacles to structural transformation. The numbers, indeed, are staggering:

- More than 1.3 billion people (almost 20 percent of the world's population) have no access to electricity.
- 768 million lack access to clean water.
- 2.5 billion do not have adequate sanitation.
- 2.8 billion cook their food with solid fuels (such as wood).
- 1 billion live more than 2 kilometers from an all-weather road.

This unmet demand for infrastructure investment in emerging and developing economies is estimated at more than US$1 trillion a year (World Bank, 2011b, and GIF website). Asia alone is projected to have a financing gap of $8 trillion dollars before 2020 (Asian Development Bank and ADBI 2009).

In Africa, power shortages are a key bottleneck. Per capita electricity consumption in sub-Saharan Africa (excluding South Africa) averages only 124 kilowatt-hours a year, hardly enough to power one light bulb per person for six hours a day. Power shortages also render firms less competitive, as do frequent water suspensions.

African officials we met over the years often expressed frustration at insufficient Western donor support on their infrastructure, which is not unrelated to the mainstream economics and the Washington Consensus that prevailed at that time. Mainstream economists tended to argue for small government, leaving most important function of providing public goods to the private sector. It is not surprising that, in light of these theories, "donors ... neglected the power sector in the 1990s" (Foster and Briceno-Garmendia 2010, p. 25). Given the narrow definition of ODA (only grant and concessional loans), it is neither effective nor sufficient in overcoming the infrastructural bottlenecks. According to Neilson et al. (2009, p. 17):

Infrastructure aid comprised an average of 29.5 percent of total development assistance from DAC bilateral donors over the period 1973–1990. Starting in 1991, however, infrastructure aid dropped off considerably relative to other sectors. Total infrastructure finance declined an average of 8.3 percent per year until 2002. Since 2000, infrastructure aid per year has constituted an average of just 9.8 percent of total DAC bilateral aid.

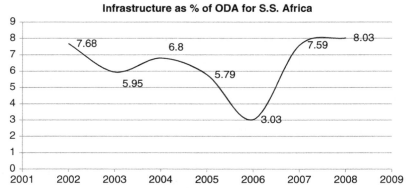

Figure 3.3 Infrastructure share in ODA, sub-Saharan Africa, 2002–2008
Source: Yan Wang's calculations based on a broad definition including all ODA in social and economic infrastructure by bilateral and multilateral organizations as a share of ODA. Basic aid data were extracted from the OECD–DAC database.

According to our calculations, the share of infrastructure in ODA to sub-Saharan Africa declined initially in the new millennium – from nearly 8 percent in 2002 to 3 percent in 2006 – but over 2007 to 2008, it showed a slight upward trend (except for 2006) due to debt-relief efforts (Figure 3.3).

Following the Gleneagles Summit in 2005, OECD development assistance placed greater emphasis on supporting African infrastructure. ODA flows almost doubled from US$4.1 billion in 2004 to US$8.1 billion in 2007. Private investment flows to sub-Saharan African infrastructure almost tripled, from about US$3 billion in 1997 to US$9.4 billion in 2006–2007. In addition, non-OECD countries, notably China and India, began to take a growing role – their commitments rose from low levels to finance about US$2.6 billion of African infrastructure annually between 2001 and 2006 (Foster and Briceno-Garmendia 2010).

From 2001 to 2010, China grew to become the largest financier of African infrastructure, accounting for 34 percent of the total (Chen 2013; Baker & McKenzie 2015). Over 50 percent of its infrastructure investment has been in electricity generation and transmission (see Chapter 5 and its annex).

On the type of financing mechanism – aid versus investment – OECD countries have appreciated the inadequacy of ODA, and their experience pointed to the direction of blended financing, combining aid and investment. In particular, the EU-Africa Partnership on Infrastructure, established in 2007, works in three levels – continental, regional, and national – and plays a key role in planning and implementing the joint EU-Africa Strategy. It finances infrastructure and supports regulatory frameworks that facilitate trade and services. The Infrastructure Trust Fund is an innovative example of cooperation among European development institutions including bilateral agencies, the European Commission, member states, and the European Investment Bank (EIB) to promote financing for regional infrastructure projects in Africa. Launched in 2006, the Fund subsidizes the financing of infrastructure projects, through a blending mechanism, mixing grants from donors with long-term investment finance from financiers. According to the 2009 Annual Report: "This blending acts as a catalyst for investment, mitigating the risks taken by the promoters and financiers and providing an incentive to consider investment in projects with substantial development impact but low financial return that could not otherwise be envisaged" (EIB 2009) Eligible projects must be based on African priorities and must be transborder projects or national projects with a regional impact on two or more countries.[7]

Consequences of the Washington Consensus for Capital Account Liberalization

Since the 1990s, many transition economies and developing countries have suffered from the Washington Consensus. Most developing countries in other parts of the world also followed the advice of the IMF and the World Bank to implement reforms to reduce government intervention and enhance the role of the market.

The result, however, was also disappointing. The economic performance of most developing countries deteriorated during this period (Barro 1998). Easterly (2001) referred the 1980s and 1990s as the lost decades for the developing countries.

The IMF's Independent Evaluation Office (IEO) admits that the IMF made mistakes during the Asian financial crisis:

The institutional view recognizes that full capital account liberalization may not be an appropriate goal for all countries at all times, and that under certain circumstances capital flow management measures can have a place in the macroeconomic policy toolkit. It has done much to change the public image of the Fund as a doctrinaire proponent of free capital mobility. (IEO 2015, p.1)

On November 14, 2012, in Kuala Lumpur, Malaysia, IEO's managing director, Christine Lagarde, stated:

[W]hile capital flows can bring great benefits, they can also overwhelm countries with damaging cycles of crescendos and crashes ... Economic management is the key. If the flows are coming through the banking system, then macro-prudential tools make sense – such as tightening conditions for housing loans or having banks hold more capital. In other circumstances, temporary capital controls might prove useful. I should point out that Malaysia was ahead of the curve in this area. (IEO 2015, p. 16)

Why did capital account liberalization become the main policy advocated by the developed countries led by the United States and the IMF after the collapse of Bretton Woods?

In a recent paper, Lin (2015c) said,

As the primary issuer of the reserve currency, the United States was the primary beneficiary of capital account liberalization in other countries. After the collapse of Bretton Woods system, the Federal Reserve began the inflation targeting policy. This meant that when capital flowed outwards and the dollar was no longer pegged to gold, the Fed could issue more money to avoid deflation and maintain economic stability. Consequently, the United States relaxed controls on capital outflows. Under that kind of situation, Wall Street became the most active promoter of capital account liberalization, because investment bankers could engage in arbitrage overseas.

Wall Street investment bankers even promoted financial liberalization, reducing regulation, and allowing for highly leveraged operations – in other words increasing the ability of financial institutions to create money, allowing them to increase the capital and profits of arbitrage. As a result, after the 1970s, the financial sector in Wall Street expanded the fastest among sectors in the United States, raking in the largest profits. In 2007, before the breakout of the financial crisis, only a small number of people were employed by Wall Street's investment banks and financial institutions, yet this minority took in 40 percent of the net profits generated by the entire U.S. economy. In 2008, after the crisis, we saw the social movement in which 99 percent of the nation protested against the top 1 percent of people in the financial sector. After the Bretton Woods system collapsed, the greatest beneficiary of capital account liberalization has been Wall Street.

Judging from Lin's experiences as Chief Economist of the World Bank, the IMF and other international development agencies have always followed the lead of the U.S. Treasury, turning from a promoter of capital account control into a doctrinaire proponent of capital account liberalization. In *Against the Consensus*, Lin discussed the above-mentioned processes and mechanisms (Lin 2013).

The theory advanced by American academia – that capital account liberalization is beneficial for the allocation of capital and economic growth in developing countries – assumes that capital is homogeneous. That is, there is no difference between financial capital and real capital. Under such a theoretical model, a currency mismatch or even a term mismatch does not exist. Nor does the asymmetry of benefits when reserve currency–issuing countries can use virtual monetary capital to exchange for real products and services from non-reserve currency–issuing countries. Developed countries and developing countries also are no different in industrial and technical structures; the only difference is in capital endowment. In such theories, capital account liberalization can be beneficial only for capital-scarce developing countries. Armed with these theories, Wall Street and international financial organizations commanded a "high moral ground" in their promotion of capital account liberalization in developing countries.

In sum, the overall effect of the collapse of the Bretton Woods system in the 1970s and the promotion of capital account liberalization by Wall Street, American academics, and the IMF was larger economic fluctuations and more frequent crises in developing countries (Lin 2015b and 2015c). After more countries liberalized their capital accounts since 1980, "there have been about 150 episodes of surges in capital inflows in more than 50 emerging market economies . . . About 20 per cent of the time, these episodes end in a financial crisis, and many of these crises are associated with large output declines (Ostry et. al 2016, p. 39).

Issues with Public Investment and Debt Sustainability

Another problem with traditional aid relates to the sustainability of debt. IEO (2007) admits that it faced the criticism that "IMF-supported programs have blocked the use of available aid to Sub-Saharan Africa through overly conservative macroeconomic programs," and that "IMF-supported programs have done little to address poverty reduction and income distribution issues despite institutional rhetoric to the contrary" (IEO 2007, p. 1). It provided a weak finding that "PRGF-supported macroeconomic policies have generally accommodated the use of incremental aid in countries whose recent policies have led to high stocks of reserves and low inflation; in other countries additional aid was programmed to be saved to increase reserves or to retire domestic debt." (IEO 2007, p. 4) And it noted, "IMF communications on aid and poverty reduction have contributed to the external impression that the IMF committed to do more on aid mobilization and poverty-reduction analysis" (IEO 2007, p. 2). This is a weak defense, in view of the many missed opportunities for poverty reduction.

In the face of rising international financing flows to Africa, some elements of the current theoretical framework may be out of date. For instance, the IMF–World Bank Debt Sustainability Framework (DSF) may be overly constraining for low-income countries because it does not take into account the dynamic impact of heavy infrastructure investment on long-term growth. In our view, the DSF fails to distinguish investment spending from consumption spending, and the time horizon is not long enough, so that the transformative impact of large infrastructure investment is not captured by debt sustainability calculations. The IMF itself admits that "a recurring criticism of the DSF is that it does not adequately capture the benefits of debt-financed public investment . . . Some argue that LIC DSFs, by failing to take sufficiently into account the assets and future income that public investment may generate, lead to overly pessimistic risk assessment, which in turn discourage potential investors while constraining how much LICs can borrow" (IMF and World Bank 2012, p. 29).

Several studies have investigated "alternative fiscal rules" that allow countries to take into account the long-term impact of pubic investment in infrastructure, distinguishing illiquidity from insolvency, and thus reducing the anti-investment bias.

- One alternative is the "golden rule," which prevents a government from running a deficit on the current account but allows it to borrow to finance (net) investment – that is, to borrow to create assets. This idea of separating the current and capital budgets is hardly new, but has been revived in the last few years.[8]
- An alternative to the golden rule that overcomes its limitations is the "permanent balance rule," which is a direct application of the inter-temporal budget constraint. Similar to consumer behavior under the permanent-income hypothesis, this rule allows a government to borrow when revenue is temporarily low or when present investment opportunities are greater than future such opportunities. This rule ensures solvency, provides a suitable treatment of productive expenditure, and avoids tax variability. In addition, it allows for the effect of initial conditions

on debt accumulation limits. Conceptually, this rule fulfills all the requirements of simplicity and transparency.

- An even more direct way to target public sector net worth is through a "net worth fiscal rule," which would set expenditure and financing decisions to achieve a desired net worth trajectory. Net worth measures and targets have featured for some time among the core principles of fiscal management in New Zealand and have also featured prominently in some proposals for reform of the European Stability Pact (Servén 2007, p. 24).

"The conventional practice of using short term cash flows to gauge the strength of public finances is deficient on several counts," according to Servén (2007, p. 25). "It amounts to equating solvency, essentially an intertemporal issue, with liquidity, which is a short term concept. This practice tends to introduce an anti-investment bias into fiscal discipline that can be, in fact, a bias against future growth, with potentially adverse consequences for public finances themselves" (Servén 2007, p. 25).

A Different Approach

The Chinese approach in Ecuador offers a good example of focusing on the long-term dynamics of a country's net worth, rather than the short-term liquidity issues in debt sustainability analysis (Box 3.2). Many developing countries have undervalued resources and land, and are facing liquidity problems and foreign exchange constraints, but are not insolvent. They can well absorb non-concessional loans for investment using their undervalued assets as collateral – for example, to build hydropower plants and alleviate power bottlenecks. In the long term, these projects can propel growth and job creation (as with Bui Dam in Ghana; see Box 8.4).

The question arises, however: How should these (undervalued) assets be valued, and in which currency? At purchasing power parity (PPP) or special drawing rights – or another measure? If one can

Box 3.2 China and Ecuador's access to international financial markets

China has recently become Ecuador's most important creditor, and seen Ecuador through a prolonged period of limited access to financial markets. In 2008, Ecuador defaulted on two outstanding bonds totaling US$3.2 billion. These two bonds amounted to less than half of all public foreign debt, and only about 6 percent of GDP (IMF 2014). Nonetheless, the default was unusual, because the government did not cite financial hardship but irregularities in the debt itself. Many international analysts opposed the default, Moody's downgraded Ecuador's debt to Caa3, and Ecuador lost access to its traditional Western creditors. This signaled an opportunity for Chinese leaders and investors to diversify their economy's sources of primary commodities through oil loans, especially as Ecuador was unable to seek funding elsewhere. China's innovative arrangements involving pre-sales of crude oil provided much-needed funds upfront.

China accounted for over one-third of Ecuador's total external public debt in 2013. It has also signed oil deals with Ecuador in which it prepays for oil shipments, giving both parties predictability in their trade.

Most loans from China are in the hydroelectric and extraction sectors, helping the government move to its goal of producing some 93.5 percent of its energy by 2021 via hydropower. But they also carry conditions to use Chinese equipment and contractors.

Moody's specifically cited Ecuador's ability to secure financing from China as a reason for upgrading its debt to Caa1 in 2012. In 2014, Ecuador re-entered international financial markets, issuing its first traditional public bond since the partial

---

Box 3.2 (*Cont.*)

default. China's share of Ecuador's external public debt fell in
2014. It appears that as of 2014, Ecuador was no longer relying
solely on China for new external financing.

Source: Ray and Chimienti 2015; and Gallagher and Myers
2014.

---

think differently, out of the box, a country's development prospects
are brighter. The DSF focuses on "what the country does not have"
(foreign exchange), not "what the country has" (unextracted) natural resources and (latent) comparative advantages. It thus has an
anti-investment bias that constrains long-term growth.

Country Ownership Is Key to Development Effectiveness

To achieve development effectiveness, aid or cooperation must be
(in donor jargon) "owned" by the developing country. One important experience from successful emerging market economies – such
as Brazil, China, and India as recipients – is that they have been
always in control of their reform and development agenda.
In particular, Chinese leaders firmly believe that "donors do not
have the full information to run the country," so they insisted that
donor programs be adapted to "meet the local conditions" (Box 3.3).

In all our discussions, African policymakers highlighted that
African leadership is key for an effective development partnership in
Africa. For African countries to be more fully in the driver's seat, as
China has been, they need greater ownership and accountability.
To achieve this, Africans need to develop their human and institu-
tional capacities to define and lead their own development processes,
crucially moving on from aid with conditionality. This hard-earned
lesson took Washington-based institutions many years to learn.

"During the late 1980s and early 1990s, the IMF played an
increasingly important role in defining overall aid policies. Its seal

---

Box 3.3 Country ownership: Donor engagement in Tanzania

Tanzania has had a bumpy relationship with development partners since the 1960s. Edwards (2014b) described former President Julius Nyerere's confrontation with the IMF on exchange rate devaluation started in 1979 – which led to a seven-year stalemate. By the 1990s, this engagement was burdening the government with the presence of a high number of both development partners and active projects associated with an estimated 2,400 quarterly reports to development partners and more than 1,000 annual development partner missions. Relationships between the government and development partners really began to fray in the 1990s over concerns about governance and public financial management, and many development partners, including the IMF and World Bank, suspended aid to the country (Furukawa 2014).

This "aid crisis" led to the adoption of the recommendations of the Helleiner Report and the creation of the Tanzania Assistance Strategy, leading to a period of aid reform. The principles included country ownership, and providing space for the government to institute policies. For example, in 2003, Tanzania introduced an annual moratorium on donor missions from April to August so that the government could focus on budgeting during that period (Roodman 2007).

Source: Custer et al. 2015, p. 25.

---

of approval was needed for other multilaterals to release their monies. Fund conditionality was controversial, as more often than not it focuses on devaluation, the elimination of subsidies, and the control of parastatals" (Edwards 2014a, p. 26).

This type of aid-with-conditionality relationship suffers from "a double principal-agent problem," where those with the greatest interest in the success of the programs – aid recipients in poor countries, and taxpayers in donor nations – are far from the decision-making process and have little information. "When the principal-agent problem is severe, officials in donor and receiving countries tend to 'capture' the aid organization, and run them according to their own interest, values, and goals" (Easterly 2003).

Jakob Svensson (2003) reported how some recipient countries behaved in a strange way:

Over the past few years Kenya has performed a curious mating ritual with its aid donors. The steps are the following. One, Kenya wins its yearly pledges of foreign aid. Two, the government begins to misbehave, backtracking on economic reform and behaving in an authoritarian manner. Three, a new meeting of donor countries looms with exasperated foreign governments preparing their sharp rebukes. Four, Kenya pulls a placatory rabbit out of the hat. Five, the donors are mollified, and the aid is pledged. The whole dance then starts again. (*The Economist*, August 19, 1995)

Svensson proposes ex post incentives for donors to reward good policies. "Instead of committing a fixed amount of aid to each recipient ex ante, and making aid conditional on reform or outcome, the donor would commit the aggregate amount to be given to a group of countries, but where the actual amount disbursed to each individual country would depend on relative performance" (p. 398). This approach raises the opportunity cost of disbursing aid ex post, and competition among recipients allows the donor to make inferences about common shocks, which otherwise conceal the recipient's choice of action. This enables the donor to give aid more efficiently (Svensson 2003).

In our view, international aid must be used in the context of a country's own development strategy, including trade and investment. The country must be able to control its reform agenda – as China has done, which we detail in the next section – and be on an equal footing with its development partners; both sides must be able to say "no." The recipient must therefore have alternative funds to draw on, either from fiscal revenue or other donors and investors, such as emerging southern partners.

China as Recipient: A Successful Partnership of Equals

As a recipient of aid, China insisted on self-reliance as the main principle in its development, drawing on lessons from its past. And for 18 years, from 1960 to 1978, China did not have domestic or foreign debt. But in 1979 it started to approach international organizations such as the United Nations Development Programme (UNDP) and the World Bank for development assistance (and, later, mutual learning – see the section "China and the World Bank: A Partnership Based on Mutual Learning" at the end of this chapter). The guiding idea seems to be what Deng Xiaoping said to World Bank president Robert McNamara: "China can develop with or without the foreign development assistance, but China can develop faster with foreign aid" (MOF and World Bank 2010, p. 7; Bottelier 2006).

Over the last 37 years, China has used a learning and experimental approach in its structural transformation and in its partnership with donor organizations. In more recent years, it has appreciated policy advice and knowledge more than capital. "The most important benefit China received from foreign aid is the introduction of new ideas, the opening of mindset, and the dissemination of knowledge," according to Kang Binjian, a director at the Ministry of Commerce (MOFCOM).[9] International development partners working in China were considered teachers who "played an irreplaceable role in China's development effort," according to Zhou Hong, a director at the Chinese Academy of Social Sciences.[10] (Zhou et al. 2015). Boxes 3.4 and 3.5 present two experiences.

China's reform agenda was generated internally by the strong desire to catch up with the industrial economies and reach the development goals set out by Deng Xiaoping. China refused to accept the Washington Consensus blindly and insisted on "finding the truth from the practices." The reform objective was to build a "socialist market economy with Chinese characteristics" through an experimental approach. This independence in ideology established China's leading role and deciding voice for its own development agenda.

Box 3.4 China as recipient: Development as learning and transformation

China's behavior as a recipient country influences its behavior as a provider of aid and development cooperation. Policymakers and practitioners in China well understand the uncertainty and the need for pragmatism in adopting measures suitable for its own country's specificities in the development and transition process.

As a recipient country, the China–donor relationship follows a pragmatic ownership model, where the developing country takes control of its development agenda, in a process of learning, selective adaptation, and innovation – starting with easier reforms from "home-grown," localized institutions such as the household-responsibility system reform in rural areas and special economic zones in urban areas, and then developing modern institutions, such as trade and investment regulations conforming with World Trade Organization rules. All learners are on an equal footing, picking and choosing what they are most interested in, from those who have appropriate knowledge or comparative advantage in providing the lessons in a manner fully consistent with the New Structural Economics, learning in a flying geese pattern.

China's development model, if it can be called that, is based on pragmatism, learning, and experiment. Understanding well the uncertainty in the development process, Chinese leaders firmly believed that "no one knows the country better than ourselves" – and that foreign donors and partners do not have the full information needed to "run the country," insisting that foreign aid must "meet local conditions" – tenets exemplified in dealings with the World Bank and Japan International Cooperation Agency from the earliest days.[11]

Source: Wang 2011a.

Box 3.5 China as recipient: Combining aid with investment

Based on the OECD–DAC definition and OECD statistics, the total sum of net disbursements (grants plus loans minus loan repayments) of ODA to China over the period of 1979–2007 was US$49 billion. Of this, US$20.5 billion was in grants and US$28.5 billion in (net) loans. The late 1980s and early 1990s saw a steep rise in ODA, the second half a decline, and another (less steep) pickup in the first years of the 21st century (Box Figure 1).

Official aid to China never exceeded 1 percent of GDP in any year. ODA received per nationally defined poor person stayed very low, at US$15–20 from 2000 to 2011, though rising as the number of poor people fell to 157.1 million in 2009. A large share of ODA is now in the form of non-transferred aid (Development Initiatives 2013).

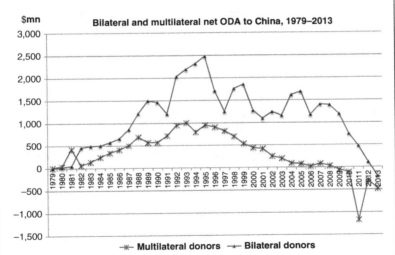

Box Figure 1 Bilateral and multilateral net ODA to China, 1979–2013 (updated) (US$ million)
Note: Net ODA may be shown as a negative number if loan repayments are higher than new ODA.
Source: Compiled from OECD/DAC data, which exclude amounts not concessional enough to qualify as ODA.

Box 3.5 (*Cont.*)

According to statistics compiled by China's National Development and Reform Commission (NDRC), disbursements of bilateral and multilateral loans (some of which were not concessional enough to qualify for recording as ODA) to China between 1979 and 2005 totaled US$83 billion. By far the largest bilateral donor to China was Japan, with more than US$20 billion in loans and more than US$6 billion in grants (at variance with OECD figures, given different definitions). The second-largest donor was Germany, with US$4.2 billion in loans and US$3.4 billion in grants between 1985 and 2007. Other donors included many OECD countries plus Saudi Arabia, Kuwait, and Russia (NDRC 2009).

More than half these investments went into transport and energy. Indeed, for the Asian Development Bank and Japan, about two-thirds of lending was directed into these sectors. Grant funding, which according to MOFCOM amounted to no more than US$6.6 billion over the 30 years before 2009, went mainly into education, the environment, rural development and poverty reduction, health, public policy, and institutional reform (MOFCOM 2009, p. 8).

Over the last three decades or so, the allocation of ODA to China has shifted from "hardware" to "software," from East to West, and from grants to loans. Partners have also changed, from relying on a government-to-government model to a many-to-many model, where the private sector and NGOs are significant. USAID, for example, has worked mainly with the private sector and NGOs.

In addition to ODA, China has benefited from large amounts of foreign loans in infrastructure (concessional and commercial loans) accounting for 56 percent of international loans

> **Box 3.5** (*Cont.*)
> borrowed from 1979 to 2005 ($142 billion of US$252 billion). In energy, China started borrowing in 1979 for the crude oil, coal, electricity, and gas subsectors, with the total reaching US$60 billion. For electricity, more than 65 percent of loans were from international commercial sources. And for oil and gas, 53 percent of the loans were from Japan's EXIM Bank and over 40 percent as international commercial loans (NDRC 2009; Kitano 2004).
> *Source:* Based on NDRC 2009 and Gransow and Hong 2009.

As a transition economy faced with huge uncertainties, China developed its own path for the transformation from a planned economy to a market-oriented economy. Although the end model may be similar to a market economy in advanced industrialized countries, from the Chinese perspective this unique path has allowed the country to maintain social stability and national security – preconditions for economic development – while building self-confidence and a favorable investment climate for foreign aid and direct investment.

China's reform started with the easier reforms, relying on home-grown localized institutions, such as household responsibility system reform in rural areas and special economic zones; the more complex reforms started relatively late: fiscal from 1994 and financial from 2000 (Figure 3.4).[12]

"Crossing the river by feeling for the stones beneath the surface" was the hallmark of economic reform. This incremental, learning-by-doing, pragmatic, and innovative approach, as reflected in all five strategies, also helped firms and institutions adjust and new entrepreneurship develop so that the private sector could outgrow the state sector.

China's broad-based growth and development may be attributed to three main elements: strong leadership and commitment for development; preference for experimentation, including piloting

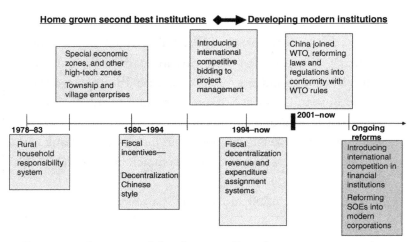

Figure 3.4 Institutional development: From home-grown to modern institutions
Source: Lin and Wang 2008, based on Wang 2005.

and scaling up home-grown, indigenous, and second-best institutions; and an open-minded learning spirit, first through learning from local ingenuity and innovation on the ground, and then nationwide collective learning from development partners and foreign investors.

China's reform and development process is still not complete. Several officials suggested to us that China is successful because it has been a good student, but it still has a lot to learn to meet current challenges.

Strategies and Principles

In receiving and managing ODA, China has insisted on the principle of self-reliance: "Use others' experience to achieve one's own objectives." Chinese leaders firmly believe that foreign donors do not have the full information needed to run the country. The government never took structural adjustment loans from the World Bank, and never borrowed under the IMF's stand-by arrangement or flexible lines of credit, because these instruments are loaded with conditions. As Pieter Bottelier, Chief of the World Bank's Resident Mission in Beijing from 1993 to 1997, put it,

The single most important thing was that the Chinese were always in charge, always "in the driver's seat." The relationship between the World Bank and most African countries was very different. . . . China very cleverly used agencies like the World Bank for their development objectives, always making sure that China itself, not the external partner, was "in the driver's seat." (Interview in June 2015)

For any ODA project, the government is the initiator, information provider, cofinancier, guarantor, negotiator, and implementer (Zhou Hong, Chinese Academy of Social Sciences). During many negotiations, the Chinese government insisted on the principle that foreign advice and technology must adapt to local conditions. Over the years, China has become an equal partner with foreign donors, and during negotiations "both sides have veto power" (Nicholas Hope, former China Country Director, World Bank). In cases where the project in question was rejected by a bilateral or multilateral donor, the government found alternative fiscal resources.[13] This strong leadership and ownership of the development agenda might be appreciated by some African countries.

Using ODA for Overall Development: Consistency with National Five-Year Plans

From the initial consultations, foreign aid programs and projects have been fully integrated with China's own development plans and their implementation. Starting with the earliest stages of reforms, China established a set of institutions for managing foreign aid.

Building Institutions for Learning and Capacity Development

China has two parallel sets of institutions: the government-administrative side with thousands of years of history and the Chinese Communist Party (CCP). They both run through central, provincial, and local levels. Promotion is based on meritocracy and is quite competitive.[14] China has built institutions to enhance human capacity for implementation: New departments and centers were established at the NDRC, MOFCOM, MOF, and LGOP to specialize in managing international projects. Project implementation units – project management offices (PMOs) in China – and project managers have bridged most misapprehensions between donors and clients. Many of the PMO officials learned from international organizations through implementing projects and were later promoted to project managers serving in China-financed projects overseas (Wang 2010).

Cofunding Mechanisms and Accountability Systems

For each development project, the government has provided cofinance, albeit in different proportions, and by different government levels. In recent years, most project proposals have come from provincial governments that committed to provide cofinancing and to be responsible for repayment of the loan. Then the central government (NDRC) approves the project according to the three criteria and national priorities, before sending details to donor agencies. This mechanism underlines the provincial government's ownership and commitment to a project and holds it accountable for implementation as well as evaluation, repayment, and follow-up. Provincial officials can be promoted if projects are implemented well, and demoted if local economic growth falls off or graft is uncovered. This mechanism also makes clear that a specific level of government (or ministry) is responsible for managing and maintaining the project (Li Xiaoyun 2013).

A Short Appraisal of ODA in China

ODA has played a catalyzing role in China's growth and poverty reduction. The Chinese people appreciate it because it has opened windows to new ideas, approaches, knowledge, and experiences, and it facilitates institutional reforms that might otherwise be blocked by interest groups.

One story illustrates this last point well. According to Pieter Bottelier:

China welcomed the Bank's conditionality as a way to improve development performance ... One of the major projects that the World Bank supported in Shanghai was the modernization of the waste water treatment system. Shanghai had very little capacity for treating the waste water, most of which went straight into the Huangpu River or the Suzhou Creek. The creation of a new water authority in Shanghai and in dozens of cities across China was World Bank conditionality. It had to set tariffs (price of water) to create its own revenue flow and finance its expenditures, from maintenance to new investment. At some point, the Shanghai government was reluctant to raise the price of water, violating the conditionality, and the project was on the verge of being suspended. The Ministry of Finance actually advised me to be "tough," and I talked with advisors to the then-Shanghai mayor. And after one day or two, they did actually raise the water price, and the project was able to move ahead. The episode actually helped the price reform in China.[15]

Learning is neither costless nor painless. China has paid a "tuition fee" for learning – by establishing institutions, offering profitable opportunities to foreign-invested enterprises and joint ventures, and accepting conditions such as "tied aid" – over half the bilateral aid to China in the 1980s and early 1990s was in this form (NDRC 2009).

Still, China learned from tied aid in the early stage of development because turnkey projects, for example, provided much-needed capital, advanced technology, and tacit knowledge. China also learned specific knowledge, managerial know-how, techniques, and systems from tied aid through technical cooperation. ODA also helped with training and capacity building through development projects and through training project management officials – knowledge transfer is literally embodied in the growing cadre of development practitioners who were trained as project managers in PIUs (Wang 2010).

China and the World Bank: A Partnership Based on Mutual Learning

At its best, the relationship between developing countries and international and bilateral development agencies is one of partnership in a learning process, on an equal footing. Learning has often been a two-way street, with for example, the World Bank learning from the country client, and the country client learning from the World Bank (Wang 2005, p. 73).

The World Bank's first official mission to China to discuss Beijing's request was led by its president, Robert McNamara, in April 1980. The mission was received by Deng Xiaoping who told the mission: "We are very poor. We have lost touch with the world. We need the World Bank [for us] to catch up. We can do it without you, but we can do it quicker and better with you." Just a few weeks later the World Bank's Board approved Beijing's request: McNamara saw a historic opportunity, but also realized that helping China reorient its development model would present enormous and unprecedented challenges for the Bank.

The relationship with the Bank quickly became very broad and deep: China became the World Bank's largest borrower and one of the largest recipients of technical assistance in the early 1990s before the program began to shrink toward the end of the decade. Between 1980 and 2010, the World Bank lent China US$47.8 billion, with 45 percent for energy and transport infrastructure (MoF and World Bank 2010. p. 46). Naturally, the nature of the relationship changed over time. China lost access to the Bank's soft-loan window (via the International Development Association) in 1999. From the late 1990s, it relied on the Bank primarily for selective technical, institutional, and conceptual innovations in development (Bottelier 2006).

China's rapid growth and poverty reduction have made it a good source of global knowledge.[16] World Bank President James Wolfensohn initiated a yearlong learning process,

"Scaling Up Poverty Reduction," in 2003 to summarize and disseminate China's experiences. For instance, in the Loess Plateau Watershed Rehabilitation Project, the World Bank's task manager learned about the utility of grazing bans from local indigenous people. The project led to such positive outcomes conducive to poverty reduction and environmental rehabilitation that the Chinese government provided an award to the task manager. In the Bank's Southwest Poverty Reduction Project, local governments in Guangxi Province initially had a poverty county–targeting approach, but the World Bank team convinced them to implement a household–participation approach. A labor mobility component was added to the project design later, on receiving demands from surveys of local poor people who wanted to find job opportunities for their sons and daughters in coastal regions. This labor mobility approach was then proven very effective for reducing poverty in the remote and inland regions, and later scaled up in poverty reduction projects all over the country.

Concluding Remarks

Nearly eight years after the global financial crisis began and subsequent protracted sluggishness, more humility is needed for all economists, including those in the Washington-based institutions. The IMF's former chief economist and director of research, Olivier Blanchard, sets a good example. He openly questioned the pertinence of the policy advice given to low- and middle-income developing countries for decades:

It was tempting for macroeconomists and policymakers alike to take much of the credit for the steady decrease in cyclical fluctuations from the early 1980s on and to conclude that we knew how to conduct macroeconomic policy. We did not resist temptation. The crisis clearly forces us to question our earlier assessment (Blanchard et al. 2010, p. 199).

The advice from the IMF and other "mainstream" economists in earlier years before the 2008 global crisis had often led to the adoption and implementation of misguided economic policies, with heavy financial, economic, social and human costs in both industrial and developing countries. These include inadequate investment in public goods such as infrastructure and special zones for promoting structural transformation, premature liberalization of the capital account, and inadequate respect for country "ownership." The impact of the "Blanchard revolution" was such that the IMF decided to subsequently revisit many important economic issues such as capital account liberalization, and other issues that were left out, including inequality, structural transformation, and gender economics (Monga and Lin 2015, p. 3). In our view, the misguided policy recommendations, at least those before 2008, led to some extent to the ineffectiveness of international aid in the last 60 years.

Notes

1. Non-transferred aid is ODA that does not represent a new transfer of resources to a developing country. This includes debt relief, administrative costs, costs of students within donor countries, costs of refugees within donor countries, and subsidies to donor country banks. Also included in this category are any other CRS records that are specifically flagged as being spent through donor-country government bodies. According to Development Initiatives (2013), at least US$22 billion (£13.7 billion) of the $100 billion-plus reported by donors as bilateral ODA in 2011 was never transferred to developing countries.
2. We thank an anonymous reviewer for pointing this out.
3. This period coincides with Edwards' planning period.
4. The development agenda was expanded in this period in order to achieve MDGs. See, for example, Thomas et al. 2000 on the quality of growth and the World Bank's World Development Reports for various years after 1999.
5. Both authors have worked closely with policymakers in Africa, although in different capacities. Justin Lin was Chief Economist of the World Bank and has traveled over 30 times to Africa to meet many heads of state and top policymakers. Yan Wang served as the coordinator of the China-DAC Study Group from 2009 to 2011, interviewed many mid-level policymakers, and participated in study tours and five conferences on such topics as development partnerships,

agriculture and poverty reduction, infrastructure investment and growth, and enterprise development. She has worked with development partners from Africa and China, OECD-DAC donors, and multilateral organizations.

6. For an overview on Aid to Africa, see Quartey and Afful-Mensah 2015.

7. Source: AFD Case Study; and EIB 2009.

8. Blanchard and Giavazzi 2004; H.M. Treasury 2002, 2004; and Servén 2007.

9. Interviewed by Yan Wang in 2009.

10. Interviewed by Yan Wang in 2009.

11. Asymmetric information is prevalent in the area of development aid and cooperation. Examples include principal-agent problems and broken feedback loops. For details, see Martens et al. 2002, Svensson 2003, and Stiglitz 1989, among others.

12. See Lin 1992, 2012b; and Lin et al. 1996.

13. For example, on the Qinghai Anti-Poverty project, after demonstrations by a pro-Tibetan Group and a prolonged period of World Bank inspections, Premier Zhu Rongji decided in 2000 to withdraw the proposal for World Bank financing and implemented the project using China's fiscal budget. See Bottelier 2001.

14. See Kenneth Lieberthal (2003) for details. In this book, we focus only on institutions relevant to developing countries.

15. Interview by Yan Wang with Pieter Bottelier, June 2015.

16. On China's achievement in poverty reduction, see Ravallion and Chen 2007.

FOUR

South-South Development Cooperation Helps Structural Transformation

---

Box 4.1 Chapter at a glance

This chapter discusses the rationale for South-South Development Cooperation (SSDC) and argues that SSDC with China and other emerging market economies is likely to bring quick wins in developing countries in poverty reduction and inclusive, sustainable growth.

Emerging economies, especially China, have comparative advantages in infrastructure sectors, including construction material industries, civil engineering, and manufacturing. They also have them in supporting improvements to infrastructure – a key growth bottleneck – through grants, loans, and other financial arrangements. Such financial arrangements are win-win for both sides of the financial flows.

Brazil, China, and India are continent-sized economies, and their emergence in the global arena has created an unprecedented opportunity for other developing countries. China, after achieving a dramatic structural transformation over the past 37 years, can provide ideas, tacit knowledge, and experience, as well as development finance and investment for

---

Box 4.1 (*Cont.*)

transformation. And, as real wages rise in China and in other upper-middle-income countries, it will relocate some manufacturing jobs, alongside some outward direct investment, to other developing countries. A key upshot is that, based on historical experience, any low-income country capturing the window of opportunity for relocating light manufacturing can have dynamic growth for several decades – generating jobs, eradicating poverty, and becoming a middle- or even high-income country.

What South-South Development Cooperation Is

The history of international development has seen two types of development cooperation: North-South and South-South. North-South cooperation, or aid, "has been based on the obligation of developed countries to assist developing countries because the former have much more resources and have also benefited from their former colonies" (Martin Khor, November 16, 2015).[1] Countries in the Organisation for Economic Co-operation and Development (OECD) have committed to provide 0.7 percent of their gross national income (GNI) as development assistance, a target that only a few countries are meeting.

SSDC, by contrast, is the exchange of resources, technology, knowledge, and expertise between developing countries, also known as countries of the global South. It is based on the principles of solidarity, mutual respect, mutual benefit, and non-interference in domestic affairs. According to the United Nations,

South-South cooperation is a broad framework for political, economic, social, cultural, environmental and technical collaboration among countries of the global South, that is excluding developed countries. Involving two or more developing countries, this may be on bilateral or other basis (e.g. trilateral, sub-regional, regional, inter-regional). Sharing of knowledge, skills, expertise and resources to meet development goals is a characteristic of this form of cooperation. Recent years have seen increased South-South trade and FDI flows, moves towards regional integration, technology transfer, sharing of solutions and expertise and other form of exchange (UN Office for South-South Cooperation).[2]

Until recently, it was seen as secondary to the large amount of North-South aid in the world of development assistance, with its established definitions, concepts, and vast literature of theoretical and empirical studies. SSDC, however, does not have consistent definitions across countries, legal or monitoring mechanisms, or large datasets. Indeed, developing country policymakers often insist that SSDC can only supplement – not replace – North-South cooperation.

In fact, the global South is now a much heterogeneous group of countries, and is no longer a homogenous "backward" group. As Nagesh Kumar stated in 2008:

Different countries and even regions within the countries are at vastly different stages of development. Thus the complementarities within the group have increased tremendously. The relevance of [SSDC] arises from the replicability of development experiences of one country in other co-developing countries. In the process of their development, developing countries accumulate valuable lessons. These skills and capacities are due to shared development challenges faced by them.

... Among the largest contributors to development cooperation were China, India, each contributing about US$ 1 billion a year, followed by Republic of Korea and Turkey contributing around US$ 500 million p.a. (Kumar 2008).

Similarly, after studying the philosophies of BRICs countries in providing development cooperation, Mwase and Yang (2012) contend that development finance for most BRICs differs from that of traditional donors in three main ways:

- BRICs, Russia aside, provide financial assistance based on the principle of "mutual benefits" in the spirit of South-South cooperation, while Russia and traditional donors emphasize the role of aid in reducing poverty.

- BRICs, particularly China, view policy conditionality as inter-
  fering with recipients' sovereignty and tend to provide non-
  cash financing as a means to circumvent corruption, while
  traditional donors view policy conditionality as a means to
  ensure efficient use of aid.
- The public investment scale-up associated with BRIC development finance has benefited low-income countries by alleviating
  key infrastructure bottlenecks, boosting export competitiveness,
  and making goods and services more affordable to consumers.
  Continued engagement with BRICs holds the potential to raise
  low-income countries' economic growth and reduce poverty in
  the long run.

However, concerns have been raised over debt sustainability, pace
of employment creation, labor practices, and competition with local
firms. While none of these concerns is uniquely related to BRIC
financing and has been debated in the past in relation to financing
from other sources, they underscore the importance of managing the
broader repercussions of the engagement between low-income countries and BRICs (Mwase and Yang 2012).

China's South-South Development Cooperation for Structural Transformation

China's SSDC has been the subject of much debate, which has
escalated in recent years.[3] Many critics seem to have forgotten that
China is big but not yet rich – it was a low-income country when it
started providing development cooperation to Asian and African
countries in the late 1950s and early 1960s. The past 60 years have
witnessed a joint learning process for economic transformation in
China and in developing countries in Asia and Africa.

China's presence in independent Africa has evolved in three
phases. First, in the 1960s and 1970s, when China was a "third
world" country that was poorer than most African countries, it

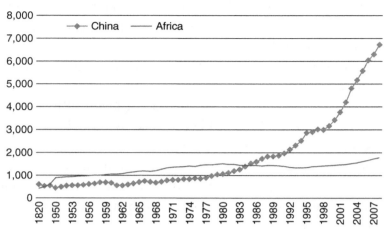

Figure 4.1 Per capita income in China and Africa (1990 international dollars)
Source: Maddison 2010.

expressed solidarity with the nonaligned movement and built major infrastructure projects like the TAZARA Railway to link Zambia's copper belt to Tanzania. In the second phase, when China returned to Africa in the 1980s and 1990s, it pursued selected investments and a more vigorous diplomatic outreach. Since the late 1990s and early 2000s China has emerged as the second-largest economy in the world. "Throughout this post-colonial engagement between China and Africa, China has represented an alternative option to the West where Africa is concerned" (Akyeampong and Xu 2015, p. 762).

Just before the new era, in 1978, China's per capita income was US$154, less than one-third the average in sub-Saharan Africa (Figure 4.1).[4] The country was inward looking as well: its trade dependency (trade-to-GDP) ratio was only 9.7 percent, with three-quarters of its exports either primary or processed agricultural products.

The Unique Features of China's SSDC

As one of the poorest developing countries in the 1980s, China has been using its comparative advantage, working with African countries to enhance their self-development capacity. Its approach to SSDC differs from the international aid of established donors, focusing on "what China owns and knows best" by combining aid, trade, and investment.

In official jargon, China follows the principles of equality and mutual respect, reciprocity, mutual benefit, and noninterference in domestic affairs. Aside from adherence to the One China principle, no political strings are attached to China's cooperation. This is not to say that China's aid or development cooperation is purely altruistic – it is not. The government "never regards such aid as a kind of unilateral alms but as something mutual" (State Council Information Office 2011). This mutual benefit is based on the simple idea of "exchanging what I have with what you have," (*hutong youwu*, or 互通有无), from which both sides can gain (as we learned from Adam Smith). And this concept of cooperation links aid and trade naturally.

The principle of "untying aid" expressed by the OECD–Development Assistance Committee (DAC) does not make economic sense because it separates aid from trade, isolating aid from market principles, from comparative advantages, and thus from mutual benefit. It also discourages the private sector's participation in development financing. Aid in the OECD definition becomes "unilateral alms" after untying aid from trade. By definition, this concept of aid gives the aid donors a moral high ground as if aid is purely altruistic, placing developing countries on the receiving end – an unequal and passive position without ownership. In contrast, African commentators have appreciated the Chinese approach of cooperation, one that has "engendered country ownership and self-reliance" (Manji and Naidu 2009, p. 7).

Based on its trade structures, some have criticized China for practicing "neocolonialism" (importing resources and exporting manufactures) in Africa and other continents, but their analysis downplays two basic facts.

First, the import–export patterns of countries are largely *endogenously determined* by their own natural and factor endowment structures. The China–Africa trade pattern is not a result of any deliberate foreign policy. What China has been doing is following its comparative advantages, and there is nothing wrong with other developing countries following their own at each stage of their transformation. As Paul Krugman and Vernables (1995) said:

Comparative advantage still explains much, perhaps most of world trade. However, both traditional location theory and recent work in economic geography generally assume away inherent differences between locations, and instead explain regional specialization in terms of some kind of external economies. (Krugman and Vernables 1995, p.4)

Trade between countries with different endowment structures due to different stages of development can be better explained by the Heckscher-Ohlin model, – that is, in simplest words, trade patterns are determined by different factor endowment structures of various trading countries. As African countries continue to accumulate factor endowments – human, physical, and financial – their export structures will transform and upgrade.

Experience has shown that trade based on comparative advantage is a more powerful engine of growth and poverty reduction than aid.[5] China is now the largest trading nation and, for many African countries, the largest trading partner. Its trade combined with aid provides demand for African goods and commodities as well as investment opportunities for job creation.

Second, China's definition of aid differs from that of the OECD–DAC,[6] so direct comparison is pointless. Indeed, it is true that there is no foreign aid law in China, and in that sense, the official/legal definition of China's foreign aid remains opaque. We think that given the One Belt, One Road grand vision and the newly established Asian Infrastructure Investment Bank (AIIB) and other development institutions, the Chinese government should strongly consider drafting a foreign aid law that would provide a clear philosophy and rationale for foreign aid and cooperation, a broader base for citizen participation, appropriate checks and

TABLE 4.1 *China's foreign aid and composition*

Dimensions	Categories
Financial resources for foreign aid	Grant
	Interest-free loans
	Concessional loans
Forms of foreign aid	Complete projects
	Goods and materials
	Technical cooperation
	Human resource development cooperation
	Chinese medical teams working abroad
	Emergency humanitarian aid
	Overseas volunteer programs
	Debt relief
Distribution of foreign aid	Agriculture
	Industry
	Economic infrastructure
	Public facilities
	Education
	Medicine and public health
	Clean energy and coping with climate change

Source: State Council Information Office 2011.

balances, better transparency, more monitoring and evaluation, and clearer accountability (see also Chapter 7).

What is the current definition? According to the State Council Information Office White Paper on China's Foreign Aid (2011), China provides grants, interest-free loans, and concessional loans, with eight types of foreign aid: "complete (turnkey) projects,[7] goods and materials, technical cooperation, human resource development cooperation, medical teams sent abroad, emergency humanitarian aid, volunteer programs in foreign countries and debt relief" (p. 8). Table 4.1 presents a classification of China's foreign aid. Other official flows (OOF) and OOF-like loans and investments are not included in the official definition of foreign aid. Braütigam (2011a) discusses these definitions.

Based on strong demand from African countries, new types of SSDC have been added in recent years, including OOFs (large but less concessional loans and export credit provided by China Exim Bank); resource-financed infrastructure packages;[8] equity investments by the China–Africa Development fund; and infrastructure investments by China Development Bank and other commercial banks (which are OOF-like loans and investments for development, but non-concessional and suitable for long-term infrastructure investment). However, these are not considered foreign aid in the current definition.

China's SSDC is small, commensurate with its per capita income. Many analysts have tried to compare the volume of ODA between China and established donors such as the United States without considering the huge differences in per capita income, which makes the exercise rather misleading.[9] When China started to provide ODA to African countries some 50 years ago, it was poorer than most of them. Even in 2014, when its per capita income was US$7,594, that was only one-fourth to one-eighth of that in established OECD donor countries (Box Figure 1 in Box 4.2).

Box 4.2 China's South-South Development Cooperation: Commensurate with per capita income and more generous than some other donors

This box considers stages of development and compares China's ODA as a share of GNI against that in OECD countries.

We use a recent estimate of China's ODA by Kitano and Harada (2014), which follows the OECD–DAC definition. It puts China's net ODA at US$7.1 billion in 2013. They then estimated the net disbursement of preferential export buyers' credit of US$7 billion that year. The two together

Box 4.2 (*Cont.*)

sum to US$14.1 billion as China's development finance (a conservative estimate). They accounted for 0.08 and 0.15 percent of GNI respectively in 2013. According to our own estimation, China's ODA as a share of GNI comes to 0.09 percent in 2014. The ratio is lower than that in some OECD countries, but on a linear regression on a scatter chart, China is well above the line, indicating that it is contributing a relatively significant proportion of its GNI as ODA relative to its per capita income of US$7,594 in 2014.

In other words, at its current stage of development, China is more generous with ODA than some rich countries.

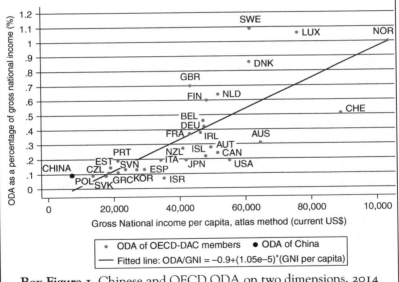

Box Figure 1 Chinese and OECD ODA on two dimensions, 2014
Source: Wang 2011a, p. 22. Updated based on AidFlow data, accessed February 2016.

Box 4.3 China's multilateral support is small, but rising

Most development cooperation from China is distributed bilaterally, but China also disburses funds to international and regional bodies as either core or earmarked contributions (US$425 million in 2010). Regional banks and United Nations agencies receive some of these contributions. China also cooperates under trilateral agreements, as with the Food and Agriculture Organization of the United Nations for food security initiatives in Liberia and Senegal, and with the United Kingdom on natural disaster preparedness and response in Bangladesh and Nepal.

China blends development cooperation with OOF instruments. Standard agreements with developing countries include a mix of aid, export credits, and export buyers' credits as well as commercial loans. Details are scant, but China's major investments are in agriculture, industrial development, economic infrastructure, public facilities, and social services. Climate change is a new area of intervention. Data on concessional loans for 2009 show heavy investment in economic infrastructure (61 percent) and industry (16 percent).

China provides relief and humanitarian aid in kind and in cash donations. Its largest contribution was in 2005 to support Asian countries hit by the tsunami. China also provides humanitarian assistance to countries in other regions. Between 2004 and 2009, it supported about 200 operations.

With the newly established AIIB and New Development Bank, China's contribution to multilateral organizations is set to climb steeply (Chapter 8).

Source: Development Initiatives 2013, p. 245.

Linking the New Structural Economics and South-South Development Cooperation

We make two propositions on the features of China's SSDC consistent with the New Structural Economics (NSE), which we believe are validated by the case studies in this and the following chapters.

Our first proposition is that a learning partner successful at transformation can use its comparative advantage in development to help diffuse tacit knowledge on the how-to issues of development. China has thousands of years of history of "learning from friends from afar," and believed in "teaching it only if you know it well" (in our context, "you can teach others only if you have a comparative advantage"). Using comparative advantage allows both partners to gain (as we know from Adam Smith), so the incentives of both partners are aligned to achieve mutual benefits or win-win. We can even measure these "gains from cooperation" just as we can measure the "gains from trade." This is fundamentally different from the "aid with conditionality" model where the incentives of donors and recipients are not aligned.

Many Chinese officials have said in interviews that "China is successful because she is a good student." It is just natural that good students, fast in learning (and having developed comparative advantage in some sectors), can help others with "what they can" (however little they have). China has been focusing on transforming "what these countries have" (endowment) to "what they can potentially do well" (latent comparative advantage) in order to achieve win-win. For example:

- In the 1950s and 1960s, China established good primary health and education systems and rapidly improved life expectancy and eliminated illiteracy. Using this comparative advantage, it has been sending medical teams, teachers, and agricultural experts to African countries for 50 years, and providing scholarships for the continent's students, in this way transmitting hand to hand tacit knowledge and experience. The feedback from Africa on Chinese

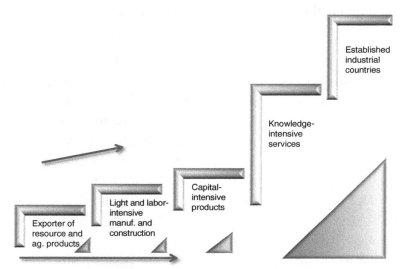

Endowment: Natural, Physical, and Human & Intangible capital

Figure 4.2 China and Africa, teammates in climbing the same mountain of structural transformation one step at a time: Following comparative advantages
Source: Authors.

medical teams is overwhelmingly positive and appreciative (see, for example, King 2013).

- China achieved high yields in agriculture, fisheries, and animal husbandry after 1979. Using this experience and comparative advantage, it has financed the construction of agricultural technical demonstration centers in Africa, transferring appropriate agricultural and aquatic technologies (Braütigam 2015). One of the earlier centers led to a sugarcane farm and the Sukala Sugar Refinery in Segou, Mali, operating since 1996. Based on its good result, the government of Mali approved an expansion (Box 4.5).

Our second proposition is that a country can learn only by moving up one tiny step at a time, reflecting its natural or accumulated factor endowments (Figure 4.2). In other words, it learns by following its comparative advantages (not defying them), based on the NSE.

Because China has conducted partial reforms gradually, it can help others with partial reforms through special economic zones (SEZs) and experiments. A country can change its endowment structure through saving, investment, and learning to accumulate natural, physical, human, and institutional capital, but it takes a long time. It is impossible for a capital-scarce country to defy its comparative advantages to leapfrog and become a capital-intensive manufacturer or a high-tech knowledge economy.

China's SSDC "engenders ownership and self-reliance" (Manji and Naidu 2009, p. 7) and encourages countries to follow their comparative advantages (the CAF approach), gradually, not to leapfrog using shock therapy because (based on its own experience) such therapy does not fit the realities of developing and transition economies. For example:

- Many Chinese firms relocating to Africa produce labor-intensive light manufacturing products – see, for example, Shen (2015), World Bank (2011a and 2012), Weisbrod and Whalley (2011) and the case on the Huajian shoe factory in Ethiopia (Chapter 6).
- Chinese technology is inexpensive and more appropriate for low-income countries. One example is the labor-intensive technology used to build the TAZARA railway (Akyeampong and Xu 2015). Another is the herbal medicine for malaria (artemisinin, also called Qinghaosu in Chinese), which has saved millions of lives. Chinese scientist Tu Youyou received the Nobel Prize in 2015 for working with a team on this medicine since the 1970s.

Another reason China cannot help others leapfrog is because of its own constraints. For instance, since China is not yet a knowledge economy, it cannot help others to become one. What most Chinese companies know best is labor-intensive light manufacturing, not capital-intensive manufacturing or knowledge-intensive services (except for Huawei, ZTE, and a few other high-tech companies). Such constraints also include labor and environmental standards:

Some Chinese firms are not in full compliance with China's own laws and regulations, and they still need to be educated and trained in these standards, so some of their overseas projects are bound to have these problems. What they need is feedback or pushback from host-country governments, NGOs, and civil society encompassing mutual learning, as well as better legal and regulatory systems in the host countries.

Africa and China are, thus, teammates climbing the same economic mountain of structural transformation, freely selected by each other. China, a bit higher up in the mountain, helps build "bottleneck-easing" infrastructure and SEZs in Africa to facilitate structural transformation, drawing on its own ideas and experiences. And with labor costs rising fast in China, African countries can benefit by attracting labor-intensive enterprises relocating outside China. Both sides gain from cooperation just as trading partners gain from trade. But good climbers may also need to be pushed up sometimes. African people, the media, and NGOs can help encourage the right behavior in their partners. Later, we propose establishing a system to rate all partners on their compliance with international standards.

The propositions and the framework encapsulated in Figure 4.2 are fully consistent with the logic of the NSE:

- All learners or partners start on an equal footing. Some learn faster. All are free to choose their learning partners.
- China has been moving up from labor-intensive sectors to more capital-intensive sectors, while many African countries remain at the stage of exporting natural resources and primary products. But China was there only recently: As late as 1984, half of China's exports were crude oil, coal, and agriculture products (see Figure 2.8). China's stage of structural transformation is the closest in distance to African countries, and thus has higher complementarity for the flying geese pattern (Chapter 2).
- China's approach of learning and cooperation encourages Africans to take tiny steps and to follow comparative advantages,

or identify latent comparative advantages in agriculture, infra-structure, and labor-intensive light manufacturing. Partial reforms through SEZs can also help in structural transformation, as shown by China's own experience (see Chapters 6 and 7).

- Partner countries need to respect each other, and to have recent intimate tacit knowledge and experiences to help in such an experimental approach because of similar endowments, similar institutional constraints, and similar human capital structures. China and Africa can complement each other well because they have different natural endowments, different comparative advantages, but similar human capital and institutional constraints.

What Is Comparative Advantage and How to Measure It?

Revealed comparative advantage (RCA) is a useful concept based on Balassa (1965). It measures whether the country has a revealed comparative advantage in a commodity that the country is already exporting (Box 4.4).

Box 4.4 A methodological note on revealed competitive advantage

RCA is calculated as follows:

$$RCA_{ij} = \frac{x_{ij} / X_{it}}{x_{wj} / X_{wt}}$$

where x_{ij} and x_{wj} are the values of country i's exports of product j and world exports of product j and where X_{it} and X_{wt} refer to the country's total exports and world total exports. Thus, if RCA is less than 1, the country has a revealed comparative disadvantage in the product, while if RCA is greater than 1, it has an RCA in the product.

Source: WITS/Comtrade.

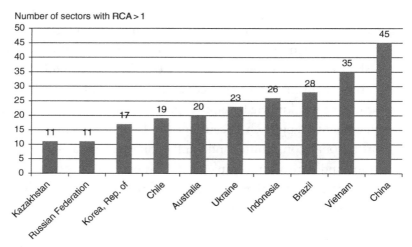

Figure 4.3 China is well positioned to help others in their transformations
Notes: The figure shows the number of sectors with an RCA > 1. Figures on the bars refer to 2010 or 2011.
Source: Authors' calculation based on World Bank, World Integrated Trade Solutions (WITS) data, HS2 1996 code, 2-digit, for 97 sectors.

Figure 4.3 shows the result for a sample of countries and sectors (out of 97 sectors) for 2010–2011. Comparing across middle-income countries, the Russian Federation and resource-rich Kazakhstan have only 11 sectors with an RCA greater than 1. Lower-income countries, such as Indonesia and Vietnam, have more sectors with an RCA greater than 1. China is the most diversified country in the group, with revealed comparative advantages in 45 of 97 sectors (with an RCA greater than 1). So it is well positioned to help other developing countries reach competitiveness in sectors where they have latent comparative advantage.

In the 1970s and 1980s, China used its comparative advantage in agriculture and light manufactures to help African countries (Box 4.5).[10] In later periods, as its manufacturing sectors became more developed, it used its comparative advantage in construction and light manufacturing and other sectors.

Box 4.5 China's green investment in agricultural processing: Transforming an aid project into an investment

China has invested heavily in Africa's agriculture and provided technical assistance. Since 2006 at least 14 agricultural technical demonstration centers have been built, and more are being set up. But China's farm investments have grown slowly.

We know of only one case in which Chinese investors have been granted – and proceeded to develop – a new area of more than 10,000 hectares of land: N-Sukala, the extension of the Sukala sugar complex in Mali, founded by a Chinese aid project in 1965. Even this was not simply "Chinese" but was a joint venture between the government of Mali (40 percent) and a Chinese company (60 percent), which took over Sukala when it was privatized in 1996. (Braütigam and Zhang 2013, p. 1690)

In March 2010, Yan Wang visited the Sukala Sugar Conglomerate, some of its sugarcane farms, and two sugar refineries, meeting Chinese and African managers and workers. The story begins like this: Mali did not have the knowledge of planting sugarcane and the ability to produce sugar in early 1960s. Some Western experts believed that the land and climate in Mali were unsuitable for sugarcane. But Chinese experts helped Malian farmers to plant sugarcane, and built two sugar refineries, in Dougabougou and Siribala, in 1965 and 1974, together known as Sukala Société Anonyme.

Initially, a turnkey aid and technical assistance project, it was returned to the government of Mali, but after returning the project suffered financial losses. In 1996, CLETC (China Light Industrial Corporation for Foreign Economic and Technical Cooperation) received a request from the Malian government to form a joint venture for industrial upgrading, which became the Sukala Sugar Conglomerate, with registered capital of 5 billion CFA francs (60 percent CLETC and 40 percent

Box 4.5 (*Cont.*)

Mali). From 1999 to 2000, the conglomerate used preferential loans from China Exim Bank for renovation, increasing daily processing capacity from 1,500 to 2,000 tons. With a total area of 100 km², the conglomerate produces 39,000 tons of sugar a year and 2.8 million liters of edible alcohol. The total assets of the conglomerate were 22.5 billion CFA francs in 2010 (Feng 2010).

Sukala Sugar Conglomerate contributed to the national economy by meeting one-fourth of market demand for sugar in Mali, and the sugar industry has become a strong sector in the country. More than 10,000 jobs were created by the project, permanent and seasonal, helping reduce poverty and raise welfare. The project also had spillover effects on other industries, promoting consumption and agglomeration of economic activities in the two towns and generating revenue for the government.

The N'Sukala Conglomerate is an expansion based on Sukala Société Anonyme's success, covering a new area of more than 10,000 hectares. This joint project, which started operations in 2012, is expected to expand sugar production more than three-fold and to satisfy all market demand for sugar and other related products, including edible alcohol. This environmentally friendly project is expected to adopt up-to-date sprinkling irrigation to cut down on water use and provide thousands of jobs.

Source: Based on Bräutigam and Zhang 2013; Feng 2010; and Sun 2011.

Notes

1. Martin Khor, "China's New South-South Funds: A Global Game Changer?" *IPSNEWs.* November 16, 2015. See: http://www.ipsnews.net/2015/11/opinion-chinas-new-south-south-funds-a-global-game-changer/.

2. For details on the characteristics and benefits of South-South Cooperation, see: http://ssc.undp.org/content/ssc/about/what_is_ssc.html.

3. See, for example, a paper by Naím 2009.

4. Unless indicated otherwise, statistics on the Chinese economy are from the *China Statistical Abstract 2010, China Compendium of Statistics 1949–2008,* and various editions of the *China Statistical Yearbook,* published by China Statistics Press.

5. The Republic of Korea; Taiwan, China; and China after 1979; and the experience of the U.S. African Growth and Opportunity Act program and the European Union's Everything but Arms initiative.

6. As seen in Chapter 1.

7. Turnkey projects and in-kind assistance were developed in the 1960s and 1970s, when China was desperately short of foreign exchange. These types of projects allowed poor countries to help each other without using dollars or other foreign exchange.

8. See World Bank 2014.

9. Studies include, for example, Wolf et al. (2013) and Strange et al. (2013).

10. More examples can be found in Braütigam 2015.

FIVE

Using China's Comparative Advantage to Address Africa's Infrastructure Bottlenecks

---

Box 5.1 Chapter at a glance

It is well established that infrastructure development contributes strongly to economic growth and poverty reduction. However, Africa's infrastructure, especially the power sector, has been neglected for too long.

As the New Structural Economics (NSE) shows, soft and hard infrastructure are both components of a country's factor endowment and thus critical to its comparative advantage and structural transformation, as it moves from what it *has* (endowment) to what it can *do well* (latent comparative advantage). We show that China has comparative advantages in building infrastructure such as highways, hydropower-dams, and most recently high-speed trains. Its experience in how it financed its rapid infrastructure growth also offers useful lessons to African and other developing countries.

China and other nontraditional development partners have made major inputs into building infrastructure in Africa, attempting to ease the growth bottlenecks and contributing directly and indirectly to job creation there. Case studies using 168 China-financed infrastructure projects in Africa support this claim.

The New Structural Economics and Infrastructure: A New Mind-Set

The World Bank estimates that annual investments of more than US$1 trillion – about 7 percent of developing country GDP – are required to meet basic infrastructure needs in the medium term. Countries that grew rapidly – such as China, Japan, and the Republic of Korea – invested upwards of 9 percent of GDP every year for decades. Assuming that infrastructure financing in developing countries continues at historical trends, an infrastructure financing gap of more than US$500 billion a year remains over the medium term.

However, investing in infrastructure alone is not sufficient to propel the growth engine and generate jobs unless it is combined with productive assets and human capital. Therefore, we argue that, based on the NSE, infrastructure investment needs to be associated with zone or urban development and structural transformation in order for it to become self-sustainable.

From Natural Endowments to Productive Assets

The NSE postulates economic development as a dynamic process that entails structural changes, involving industrial upgrading, which increases labor productivity, and corresponding improvements in "hard" (tangible) and "soft" (intangible) infrastructure, which reduce transaction costs, at each level of development. Such upgrading and improvements require coordination, with large externalities to firms' transaction costs and returns to capital investment. Thus, in addition to assuring an effective market mechanism, the government should actively facilitate structural transformation, diversification, and industrial upgrading (Lin 2012e, p. 14–15).

Investment in appropriate infrastructure and industrial assets would increase the value of land (a commonly acceptable principle). Land-based financing offers powerful tools that can help pay for urban infrastructure investment.[1] These options have been explored during China's experimentation on special economic zones (SEZs) and the infrastructure around these zones (Wang 2011a).

Therefore, our first proposition is that:

Other things being equal, a piece of land with the proper level of infrastructure *is always more valuable than a piece of land without. Thus it can be well used as collateral for infrastructure development loans.*

This proposition is confirmed by empirical evidence that infrastructure benefits the poor because it adds value to land or human capital and reduces inequality.[2] And because infrastructure is often sector-specific, the "proper" level of infrastructure must be affordable to the population and consistent with the country's existing or latent comparative advantage. Thus the market mechanism should be relied on to have the right relative prices and to determine which infrastructure is bottleneck easing. In addition, the government must perform the functions of providing information, identifying comparative advantages and the associated infrastructure, and developing SEZs to attract domestic and international investors and facilitate the scale-up of self-discovery by the private sector.

The role of SEZs has been well accepted and proven by the successful experiences of emerging markets. In particular, SEZs can pragmatically provide a bundling of public services in a geographically concentrated area; improve the efficiency of limited government funding/budgeting for infrastructure; facilitate cluster development or the agglomeration of certain industries; and propel urban development and the conglomeration of services. They have been shown to be conducive to growth, job creation, and income generation.

Our second proposition is therefore to link infrastructure with industrial upgrading and SEZs:

Transformative infrastructure helps link a country's endowment structure with its existing and latent comparative advantages, and translate them into competitive advantages in the global market. Thus it can be made financially viable.

In other words, combining infrastructure building with industrial upgrading, as well as real estate development, can help make both

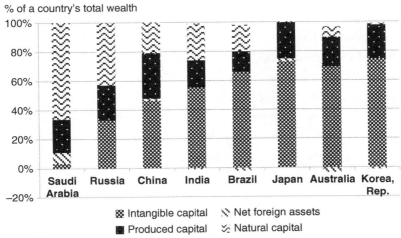

% of a country's total wealth

Figure 5.1 Transforming natural endowments to productive assets
Note: Intangible capital includes human and institutional capital.
Source: Authors based on data from World Bank 2011c.

financially sustainable. This approach potentially has high rates of return.

Based on these two propositions, any low-income country has the ability to pay for its infrastructure in the long term – if it develops a strategy consistent with its comparative advantages. The World Bank and other development banks should try to help transform "what these countries have" to "what these countries can potentially do well" (Figure 5.1).

In the long term, if a country develops industries (and the specific infrastructure needed for those industries) according to the comparative advantage determined by its endowment structure, it will have the lowest factor and transaction costs in its production in the world, become most competitive, generate the most profits (surplus), have the largest savings, and have the fastest upgrading of endowment structure. That will build the foundation for upgrading and diversifying industries to more capital-intensive industries – a virtuous circle, potentially making infrastructure financially sustainable.

Comparatively, investing in the infrastructure of developing countries could have rates of returns ranging from zero to over 100 percent (Bai et al. 2006; Canning and Bennathan 2000; and World Bank estimates). We have compared some estimated rates of return from infrastructure with the benchmark U.S. 10-year bond yields (at around 2 percent). In the current low-yield environment, more and more sovereign wealth funds, government agencies, and pension funds are seeking higher risk-adjusted returns. And they are more likely to invest in an infrastructure investment bank or, say, the Global Structural Transformation Fund proposed by Lin and Wang (2013). Recent evidence suggests that private infrastructure investment funds have higher rates of returns than private equity funds.[3] With appropriate arrangements, the excess capacity and excess saving in the high-income countries and emerging market economies can be channeled to invest in developing countries' SEZs and other bottleneck-releasing infrastructure. Such investments are win-win for both groups of countries as they generate jobs, revenues, growth, and poverty reduction in the host countries and good returns to investors (Figure 5.2).

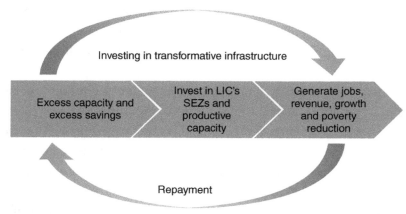

Figure 5.2 Investing in transformative infrastructure is financially sustainable
Source: Authors.

China Has a Comparative Advantage in Infrastructure, and Uses It to Help Others

Development is a process of learning, selective adaption, and innovation. Over the years, China has developed comparative advantages in construction, learning from donor-financed projects and accumulating experiences in domestic construction projects, including hydropower generation (Box 5.2) and later transport, especially highway and railroad construction (Box 5.3).

Box 5.2 China's comparative advantage in infrastructure: Hydropower

China is the world's largest producer of renewable energy, and hydropower is one of its dominant clean energy sources. Over 281.5 GW of hydroelectric power are installed domestically, making it the largest hydropower-producing country in the world, even though just 6 percent of the country's power comes from hydropower. The government has signaled its intention to increase hydropower capacity to 290 GW by 2015 (KPMG 2014).

In 2013, China's hydro-installed capacity increased by 28.8 GW to 260 GW, with a further 1.2 GW of pumped storage commissioned to reach a total of 21.5 GW. Total investment in hydropower of RMB 124.6 billion (US$20 billion) that year was roughly the same as for the previous year (IHA 2013). China now has more installed pure hydropower capacity than the next three countries combined (Brazil, United States, and Canada).

China has a demonstrated comparative advantage in exporting construction services in hydropower, including design, engineering, and implementation, based on existing domestic capacity of hydropower, built by Chinese companies; lower cost

Box 5.2 (*Cont.*)

of workers, engineers, and site foremen (Box Figure 1); ability to bring financiers to these projects; and large hydropower projects implemented in Africa and the rest of the world.

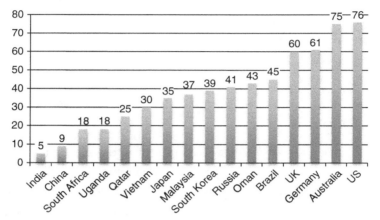

Box Figure 1 Average hourly labor cost in construction, site foremen (PPP $ 2013)
Source: Based on labor cost data from *International Construction Cost Survey* 2013.

According to China's development experience, infrastructure has played a major role in accelerating growth and poverty reduction. A popular saying is, "If you want to become rich, construct roads first."

China's infrastructure development was initially led by rapid trade expansion in the coastal regions, and financed by all levels of government as well as the private sector, with cost-recovery principles and practices widely applied. The government played a leading role in strategic planning, financing infrastructure development, and resolving the bottlenecks for growth, while maintaining fiscal discipline. Commercial loans, infrastructure bonds, and urban development funds enforced market discipline. International partners

Box 5.3 China's comparative advantage in infrastructure: High-speed railway construction

In the last 10 years, China has introduced and studied foreign technology, and gradually developed its comparative advantage in high-speed rail systems. Our 2008 paper documented this learning and innovation process. Each year, China sends many official delegations for study tours. For example, to learn the technology related to the high-speed trains from Siemens, 97 delegations or groups with 580 technicians were sent to Germany in 2006 and 2007. On April 11, 2008, China produced its first CHR3 high-speed rail locomotives. CHR300–700s are now used widely, with a top speed of 350 km per hour (Lin and Wang 2008).

China has the world's longest high-speed railway (HSR) system with over 19,000 km of track in service as of December 2015.[4] China built this HSR network, remarkably, in under 10 years at unit costs lower than for similar projects in other countries. The HSR network operates with high traffic volumes on its core routes, and with good reliability. This has been accomplished at a cost which is at most two-thirds of that in the rest of the world, showing its comparative advantage.

Several factors influence the cost of an HSR and 200 km per hour construction. The major factors are the line design speed, type of tracks, topography,[5] weather conditions (such as very low temperature requiring special design features for the road bed), land-acquisition costs (high in dense urban areas), use of viaducts instead of embankments, construction of major bridges across wide rivers, and construction of mega stations. According to Gerald Ollivier, a World Bank Senior Transport Specialist and co-author of the technical note:

Box 5.3 (*Cont.*)

Besides the lower cost of labor in China, one possible reason for this is the large scale of the high-speed railway network planned in China. This has allowed the standardization of the design of various construction elements, the development of innovative and competitive capacity for manufacture of equipment and construction and the amortization of the capital cost of construction equipment over a number of projects.

Based on experience with World Bank–supported projects, the Chinese cost of railway construction is about 82 percent of the total project costs mentioned earlier.[6] China's HSR with a maximum speed of 350 km per hour has a typical infrastructure unit cost of about US$17 million–21 million (RMB 100 million–125 million) per km, with a high ratio of viaducts

BOX TABLE 1 *Range of average unit costs (RMB million per km of double track)*

Element	350 km/h	250 km/h	200 km/h
Land acquisition and resettlement	4	5–9	5–8
Civil works	57	56–62	42–43
Embankment	24	31–42	23–28
Bridges/viaducts	71	57–73	59–62
Tunnels	–	60–95	51–68
Track			
Track (ballast-less)[a]	10	10–13	
Track (ballasted)[a]			5–7
Signaling and communications	5	3	3–4
Electrification	6	4–5	4

a. Ballast-less slab track is used for 350 and 250 km/h PDLs, ballasted track for 200 km/h railways.
Source: FSR/PAD for projects.

Box 5.3 (*Cont.*)
and tunnels. The cost of HSR construction in Europe, having design speeds of 300 km/h or above is estimated at US$25–39 million per km. HSR construction costs in California (excluding land, rolling stock, and interest during construction) is put as high as US$52 million per km.[7] Based on D.P. Crozet, the unit cost for four HSR lines under construction in France in 2013 was in a range of US$24.8–35.2 million per km.[8]

Source: Ollivier et al. 2014.

---

played a catalytic role in China's process of learning, reforming, and innovating, and they initially provided substantial funding and management experience.

China's Experience in Financing Its Infrastructure

China has used three major channels for infrastructure financing: direct budget investment from fiscal resources; market-based financing including borrowing with land-based financing; and public–private partnerships for infrastructure (PPPI).

As national policy, the government has encouraged the banking sector to finance infrastructure investment, especially in highway construction and urban infrastructure. The "user pays" principle is well applied in China, and cost recovery can reach as much as 30–40 percent of the total cost in some subsectors. Cost recovery has imposed market discipline on owners and contractors, allowed private participation, and enhanced efficiency. In 2008, for example, roughly 40 percent of urban infrastructure came from fiscal sources (including land revenue), 30 percent from bank loans, and 29 percent from enterprises (based on income streams such as fees and charges). Only 1 percent was from foreign investment and bonds.[9]

Private participation in infrastructure (PPI) in China has taken various forms (see Box 5.4). In the 1990s, the government was eager

Box 5.4 Public–private partnerships for infrastructure and private participation in infrastructure in China

In the early 1990s, rapid trade expansion and growth created growth bottlenecks in roads and power, especially in coastal regions next to the SEZs. Part of the response was to bring in the private sector, to a greater or lesser degree.

Guangzhou-Shenzhen-Zhuhai expressway. Opened in July 1994, this was the first joint-venture project with the private sector. Guangdong Highway Construction Company cooperated with Hong Kong Hopewell Holdings Ltd. to jointly finance it. The expressway was designed and built by the Hong Kong engineer and property developer Gordon Wu. With rapid economic and trade growth, the expressway became one of the busiest expressways in China. The joint venture is profitable, and this approach has been replicated elsewhere (Hopewell Holdings website: www.hopewellhighway.com/WebSite_en/ir/doc/HHI_Guangzhou_Shenzhen_Eng.pdf).

Citong bridge of Quanzhou, Fujian. This project was the first large transport infrastructure project initiated by private enterprises with a total investment of RMB 250 million. A BOT development, 15 private firms jointly established Celebrities Company, which then cooperated with Quanzhou government to establish a joint-venture company of Quanzhou Citong Bridge Development Co. Ltd. with registered capital of 60 million RMB, with Celebrities Company holding 60 percent of the shares and Quanzhou government the balance. The bridge began operations in December 1996. The "Citong mode" is a "model work" of domestic private investors participating in infrastructure construction, according to Guo (2009).

Laibin B power project. The first state-approved international BOT project in China, it is in one of the poorest regions in

Box 5.4 (*Cont.*)

China – Laibin county, Guangxi. It involved design, financing, construction, procurement, operation, maintenance, and transfer of a 2 x 360MW coal-fired power plant, at an estimated cost of US$600 million. After international competitive bidding, a consortium of Electricité de France (EDF) and GEC Alstom won the concession in 1996 (among five other short-listed competitive tenderers) with the strong backing of France's export-credit agency, COFACE. Laibin B is underpinned by three main contracts: the concession agreement, power purchase agreement, and fuel supply and transportation agreement. The government provided a letter of comfort rather than a guaranteed rate of return, thus sharing risks with the firms. These documents absorbed the experiences of BOT contracts from other countries and the current situation in China. The project is running smoothly with stable electricity supply, and the Guangxi government is satisfied with it (Wang and Ke 2008 p. 126–140).

Other cases of PPPI include Xiamen Airport, Beijing Airport Expressway, Jing-Tong Expressway, Hangzhou Bay Sea-Crossing Bridge, and most recently Beijing Subway Line 4, which was started in 2004 and completed in 2009.

Source: Based on Guo 2009; and Wang and Ke 2008.

to grant favorable concessions to attract foreign investment and piloted build-operate-transfer (BOT) projects from 1996. Many varieties of BOT were invented and applied. But 1998–2004, the number of BOT and PPI projects declined, in part due to large issues of infrastructure bonds, rising land-lease revenues, and a greater number of urban development and investment companies (UDICs). Recently, as the government has tightened control of local investment platforms because of mounting local government debt, the PPPI approach has become more common.

The Rationale for Building Infrastructure "Ahead of Time"

The authors' World Bank colleagues were often amazed by the great achievement obtained by the Chinese in planning and building critical infrastructure, such as huge reservoirs, hydropower stations, national highway systems, and recently, a high-speed railway system. They were astounded partly because these investments were sometimes hard to justify purely on the basis of World Bank cost-benefit analysis (the conventional demand-based approach).

But what is the economic rationale for building infrastructure "ahead of time," as China has often done? Our hypotheses are

Proposition 1: In a fast-growing economy like China, where the costs of labor and land are rising sharply, building a highway now is much less expensive than building it 10 years later. The same may be applied to developing countries where populations are growing and urbanizing rapidly.

Proposition 2: Critical infrastructure is a public good with positive externalities. The World Bank's cost-benefit analysis is inadequate for accounting for the spillover effect of the public good, especially in considering the scale economies of, for example, a transport network in a large country or a subcontinent.

Good transport infrastructure lowers the costs of doing business across production sectors, helps consolidate fragmented markets, increases cross-border trading, and promotes competition. This infrastructure needs to be ready just when the economy needs it: Delays translate into lost economic benefits and much higher costs of acquiring land and building at a later date. Another problem with the conventional demand-based approach is that infrastructure construction starts late and operations begin much later than needed, at the cost of huge benefits to the economy and to users. And land value rises with urbanization. So, for trade facilitation and connectivity, it is vital to decide on transport infrastructure early, as China has done.

China has invested extensively and built a vast transport infrastructure quickly. In many places the infrastructure was built "ahead of time" in the expectation that "the supply of road infrastructure will create its own demand."[10] The transport infrastructure helped move people and goods across regions and counties, expanding markets and trade and serving as a catalyst to development, growth, and prosperity. The methodology for justifying projects and investments in this scenario is, however, very different from the conventional cost-benefit analysis used for projects at the World Bank.

Missing the Boat? A Comparison of Highway Unit Costs 8–12 Years Apart

In the Chinese model, close cost evaluation and due diligence are required to support and satisfy investors and the government, especially as securing finance is one of the major challenges. Here, focusing on highways, we present the type of data on cost estimates that policymakers and planners need, comparing the unit costs of highway construction in Central Asia at very roughly a decade apart.[11]

In the World Bank's analysis, the cost components of constructing 1 km of road (2- or 4-lane, asphalt or concrete) are labor, materials, and equipment. The cost of acquiring the land (for right-of-way)[12] is not included, because it is assumed that this cost is borne by the government through the budget.[13] Given this important omission, the World Bank's advice on when to build or not to build certain highways should be re-evaluated by the government, because the land price could be prohibitively high near urban centers.

Without the land cost, the unit cost of 1 km of highway in 2012 was twice the unit cost in 2000 (Table 5.1). If the price of land is rising, especially near urban corridors, the justification for planning highways ahead of time is even stronger. The table presents costs per kilometer for a number of projects in the Western Europe–Western China International Transit Corridor (WEWC) through Central Asia and, as baseline comparators, average costs for projects in South Asia, as well as a world average in 2000.

The prices of labor, material, and equipment are rising; land-acquisition costs increase faster but at different speeds depending on

TABLE 5.1 *Highway construction costs 8–12 years apart (US$ million per km)*

Pavement type, new construction	WEWC 2012	WEWC 2009	WEWC 2008	South Asia (average) 2000	World (average) 2000
4-lane, cement concrete	4.40	4.22	3.50	2.21	2.89
4-lane, asphalt concrete				2.97	2.49
2-lane, cement concrete		2.30		N/A	1.02
2-lane, asphalt concrete			1.60	1.00	1.06

Source: Prepared by Manzoor Rehmen based on published reports from the World Bank.

Notes: Road categories are based on former Soviet Union Road Design Standards (SNiP). Category I: 4 lane (2 × 7.5 m), formation width 28.5 m; Category II: 2 lane (2 × 7.5 m), formation width 15 m. Concrete pavement 28 cm, asphalt pavement 29 cm. The design life (for calculating the internal economic rate of return) is 20 years. Physical contingencies are included.

the region, ranging from 5 percent to 50 percent or more a year (indicated by different studies). For skilled labor, which is already in short supply, the situation seems worse, given that more "megatransport" projects are planned.

The Chinese model of building transport infrastructure ahead of time therefore makes sense, given land-acquisition constraints (availability and cost), rising costs of labor and material, and increasing scarcity of skilled labor. This approach may, however, be more applicable for international, cross-border, or national corridors rather than national, provincial, or rural road networks.

How China's Development Cooperation Helped Address Africa's Bottlenecks

Nontraditional bilateral development financiers such as China, India, Arab countries, and Brazil have emerged as major financiers of infrastructure projects in Africa (Box 5.5).

Box 5.5 Southern partners are leading financiers of infrastructure in sub-Saharan Africa

A 2013 study ranks the donors or providers of infrastructure in sub-Saharan Africa for 2001–2008. China is the largest, followed by three multilateral organizations: The International Development Association (IDA), European Commission (EC), and African Development Fund (AfDF). Three southern providers are in the top 10: China, India, and the Islamic Development Bank. China alone accounts for 34 percent of total official financing on infrastructure in sub-Saharan Africa – higher than any northern partner (Chen 2013), a point backed up by a Baker & McKenzie study (2015), which found that China is "by far the largest investor in African infrastructure."[14]

China-based development financial institutions are estimated to be the largest single source of funding, contributing over US$13.4 billion in Africa in 2013 alone (Box Figure 1), according to the Infrastructure Consortium for Africa, and almost US$60 billion over the period covered (Baker & McKenzie 2015). Over 2001–2010, most Chinese financing commitment went to electricity, information and communications technology (ICT), and transport in sub-Saharan Africa (Box Figure 2). Electricity alone accounted for 50 percent by value (Chen 2013).

"What's notable is the evolution of Chinese investment to a sophisticated approach after learning from early experiences," said Wildu du Plessis, Head of Banking and Finance at Baker & McKenzie South Africa. "We're seeing complex projects being signed, financed, and built, including multi-billion-dollar rail projects in Nigeria and Zimbabwe as

Box 5.5 (*Cont.*)
China's One Belt, One Road policy gains traction" (Baker & McKenzie 2015).

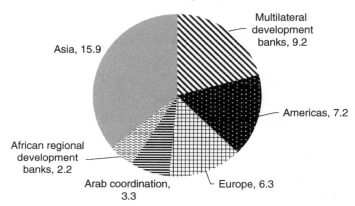

Box Figure 1 Sources of funding for African infrastructure, 2013 (US $ billion)

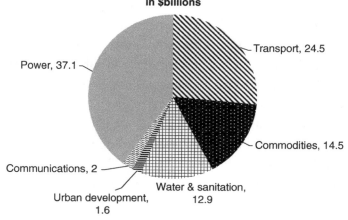

Box Figure 2 Development financial institutions' commitment by sector, 2009–14 ($ billion)
Source: Baker & McKenzie 2015.

China works particularly in bottleneck-easing sectors, such as power generation and transmission. According to Foster and Briceno-Garmendia (2010, p. 25), "donors have neglected power since the 1990s." In contrast, China allocated half its commitment to infrastructure to electricity during 2001–2010. Chen (2013) also found that China has contributed (and is contributing) 9.0 GW of electricity-generating capacity, including completed, ongoing, and committed power projects.[15] The impact of this investment is likely to be transformative when one considers that the entire installed capacity of the 47 sub-Saharan countries (excluding South Africa) is 28 GW.

China's development cooperation is concentrated in hydropower generation and transmission, in part because of its demonstrated comparative advantage (see Box 5.2). Again, China is using the approach of "do what they know best."

According to the "China's Foreign Aid" white paper, 61 percent of all concessional lending was in economic infrastructure (State Council 2011). From 2010 to May 2012, China approved concessional loans worth US$11.3 billion for 92 African projects. For example, the Addis Ababa-Adama Expressway of Ethiopia and the Kribi Deep-Water Port of Cameroon were both funded by concessional loans from China. Some of China's main commercial banks have also started buyer's credit businesses in Africa, supporting the power grid in Ghana, hydropower stations in Ethiopia, a west–east expressway in Algeria, and other projects (MOFCOM 2013).

All these are examples of China-financed infrastructure projects to ease bottlenecks. But to get back to the title of this section, have they been successful? In short: yes, two-thirds of the time. The annex shows that the majority of 168 projects in 2001–2010 targeted and helped address African bottlenecks in five sectors: water, electricity, road and rail, air transport, and telecoms (based on World Bank-PPIAF Chinese projects database). The probability of these projects in helping to ease the bottleneck was 62.5 percent. There is, however, much room for better targeting and improvement, especially in water.

Lin Launches Debate on Infrastructure
at the World Bank in 2009

When Justin Lin accepted his appointment as chief economist at the World Bank in 2008, the global financial crisis was coming to a head. Four months after his arrival in Washington, D.C., a full-blown global financial crisis started in the United States and spread rapidly to all corners of the world. After contemplating the global macroeconomic situation and the experience of East Asian countries, especially those of China in the 1997–1998 Asian financial crisis, he suggested that we have to "go beyond Keynesianism" and proposed at the Peterson Institute of International Economics in February 2009 in Washington, D.C., to have a "globally concerted fiscal policy to invest in infrastructure of developing countries – a Global Infrastructure Initiative."

He made his second speech on this in March 2009 at a Global Policy Seminar chaired by Yan Wang. He reiterated this view in a lunch speech at American Foreign Relations in May, which was later published in *Harvard International Review*.[16] Lin promoted this idea in several review articles or books,[17] and worked with Yan Wang on a paper "Beyond the Marshall Plan: A Global Structural Transformation Fund," which was published in May 2013 in a contribution to the UN's Post-2015 initiative.[18]

However, the response from his World Bank colleagues was lukewarm. In some internal meetings where his proposal was debated, some said that infrastructure should be left to the private sector, and others felt that Japan's experience had proven that investing in infrastructure could lead to waste and onerous debt burdens.

Nearly eight years after the global crisis began, the global economy has been through the most tumultuous times since the Great Depression. Despite the coordinated policy response of the G-20 nations for expansionary monetary policy, the global economy, especially in Europe and Japan, has not fully recovered. Having seen sub-par recovery, more and more economists agree on the need to invest in infrastructure and global public goods, including Larry Summers. The IMF also belatedly recognized, "Now it is the time to promote infrastructure development" (IMF 2014, Chapter 3).[19] But isn't its conversion too late?

Annex 5.1 China-Financed Infrastructure Projects Helped Ease Africa's Bottlenecks Almost Two-Thirds of the Time

It is well accepted that certain types of infrastructure are public goods/services and semipublic goods/services, and addressing bottlenecks in them could have large positive externalities, and hence, significant developmental impact. In this case study, we attempt to use a three-step method to address the question that whether, and to what extent, China-financed infrastructure projects match African's bottlenecks? A short answer is that they seem to have matched in nearly 63 percent of the 168 infrastructure projects in 2001–2010.[20]

Step 1

Five indicators from the World Bank database are used to define Africa countries' bottlenecks, including water, electricity, roads and rail, air transportation, and telecommunication. The year before the global financial crisis 2007 is selected because the investment decisions were made five or more years before the project implementation. These indicators include:

Sector 1 = Improved water source (percentage of population with access), 2007

Sector 2 = Electric power consumption (kilowatt hour (kWh) per capita), 2007

Sector 3 = Road sector energy consumption per capita (kilograms (kg) of oil equivalent), 2007

Sector 4 = Air transport, registered carrier departures worldwide, 2007

Sector 5 = Mobile cellular subscriptions (per 100 people), 2007.

These five sectors are selected because water (Sector 1) is largely a public good/service with large externalities for the health of the population, whereas telecom is a private service, and Sectors 2 to 4 are largely semipublic goods/services.[21]

1. First, we rank each of the five indicators/sectors from low to high and figure out the ranking number of the African country i, in sector j, denoting the ranking number as $R_{i,j}$.

2. Second, we compare the ranking numbers for Sectors 1 to 5 for the country, i, and select the lowest ranking sector to be the Bottleneck 1 for country i; and then exclude the selected sector $j*$, select the next lowest ranking sector as Bottleneck 2, and continue to follow this process for Bottleneck 3.

   This process can be expressed as,

   Bottleneck 1 for country i = $\min(R_{i,j})$, where $j = 1, \ldots 5$.

   Bottleneck 2 for country i = $\min(R_{i,-j*})$ where $j = 1, \ldots 5$.

3. Because some data are missing, we only use the countries with values in the sectors and take the average and standard deviation of each indicator. Then the bottleneck sectors are mostly below the average for that indicator j across countries.

4. For some countries the bottleneck cannot be identified as (i) the country is ranked high in all five sectors (such as South Africa), or (ii) they are countries too small to have enough data values such as roads, rail, and air transport.

Step 2

World Bank-PPIAF Chinese projects database is used to find the location and number of infrastructure projects financed by China in each sector during 2001–2010. There are 168 projects allocated in, originally, four sectors. Here we divide the transport sector into two sectors, with rail and roads as Sector 3, and air transport as Sector 4. After re-defining this way, the five sectors are identical with the sectors in the dataset on bottlenecks.

The above two steps are conducted independently by two research assistants.

Step 3

The two datasets are merged by country code, and see if the locations of the China-financed projects match that of the bottlenecks (Figure A5.3). We have also calculated some probabilities of projects "hitting" the bottlenecks.

- Probability of (hitting one of the 3 bottlenecks) = (number of matches)/total projects
- Probability of (hitting the Bottleneck 1) = (number of hitting B_1)/total
- Probability of (hitting the Bottleneck 2) = (number of hitting B_2)/total
- Probability of (hitting the Bottleneck 3) = (number of hitting B_3)/total.

Results are:

- Probability of (hitting one of the 3 bottlenecks) = 105/168= 0.625
- Probability of (hitting the Bottleneck 1) = 39/168 = 0.232
- Probability of (hitting the Bottleneck 2) = 31/168 = 0.185
- Probability of (hitting the Bottleneck 3) = 35/168 = 0.208.

In sum, the overall probability of China-financed infrastructure projects hitting the bottlenecks is 0.625, although the cross-sectoral variation is large. Based on this result, we conclude that China's infrastructural investments in sub-Saharan countries match these countries' bottlenecks relatively well. In other words, China has contributed to easing some of sub-Saharan Africa's bottlenecks by meeting unmet demand.

There is, however, still plenty of room to improve relevance, or matching supply with specific demand, especially in the water sector, where the total investment is still very low relative to demand (Figures A5.1–5.3).

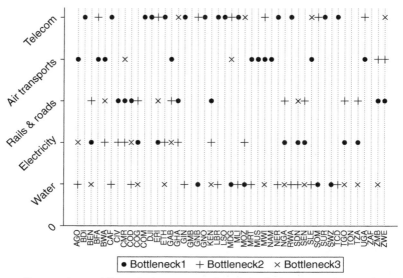

Figure A5.1 Africa: Infrastructure bottlenecks by sector (Step 1)
Source: Authors. See explanations above on Step 1.

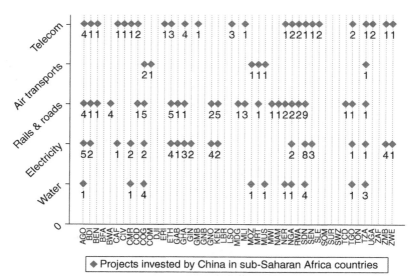

Figure A5.2 Number of China financed projects in each sector, 2001–2010 (Step 2)

Notes: Numbers in the chart are the number of China-financed infrastructure projects in that particular sector *j* and country *i*. The total number of projects is 168. Sectors are identical to those in Figure 5.6.

Source: Authors based on World Bank-PPIAF Chinese projects database.

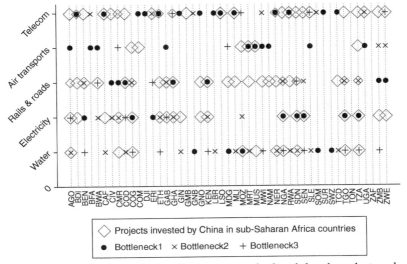

Figure A5.3 Are China-financed projects matched with bottlenecks in sub-Saharan Africa? Yes, in 62.5 percent of the projects in 2001–2010 (Step 3)
Source: Authors, by merging the two steps above using country code.

Notes

1. For legal and typical land-asset based infrastructure financing, see policy note by Peterson 2008.
2. Estache et al. 2002; Estashe 2003; and Calderón and Servén 2010a, 2014.
3. Preqin Global Infrastructure Report 2015, available online at https://www .preqin.com/docs/reports/2015-Preqin-Global-Infrastructure-Report-Sample-Pages.pdf.
4. China defines HSR as any railway in China with commercial train service at the speed of 200 km/hour (124 mph) or higher. By this definition, China has the world's longest HSR network, with more than 19,000 km of track in service by December 2015.
5. In particular, mountainous areas require extensive tunneling and bridge construction, which can reach as high as 80 percent of the alignment length.
6. Including civil works, track works, regular stations, yards, signaling, control and communication, power supply and other superstructure components; excluding the cost of planning, land, some of the mega stations, rolling stock, and interest during construction.
7. California HSR Authority, Draft Business Plan 2014, available at http://www .hsr.ca.gov/about/business_plans/draft_2014_business_plan.htm.

8. International Transport Forum, December 2013, available at http://www.internationaltransportforum.org/jtrc/DiscussionPapers/DP201326.pdf.

9. Interview with Qin Hong, Center for Urban and Rural Development, 2010.

10. "China's Pivot West." Presentation by Pieter Bottelier, at the World Bank, February 27, 2015.

11. The authors are grateful to Manzoor Rehman, Senior Project Manager at the World Bank (retired) for preparing this technical note for our book.

12. A right-of-way is the land that a highway is built on. It includes the land needed for anything that is part of the highway, such as ditches, back slopes, bridges, and culverts.

13. Mr. Rodrigo Archondo-Callao, Senior Highway Engineer and the top expert of Highway Design Manual-4 (the software for estimating costs and economic analysis) of the World Bank, has confirmed this point as below: "I have never seen the land cost being presented in our main Bank documents (PAD, ICRS, ISR) or civil works contracts, typically they are paid by the government funds (through internal transfer). Therefore, I have no information about land costs for road works."

14. See also Baker & McKenzie, www.bakermckenzie.com/news/Over-300bn-since-the-financial-crisis-Development-Capital-revealed-as-largest-funders-of-infrastructure-in-Africa/.

15. The Hoover Dam in Colorado, by comparison, is a 2 GW facility, producing electricity for about 390,000 homes (Chen 2013).

16. See Lin 2009a.

17. Lin 2011a; Lin and Doemerland 2012; and Lin 2013.

18. Lin and Wang 2013.

19. www.imf.org/external/pubs/ft/weo/2014/02/pdf/c3.pdf.

20. Lin and Wang 2013. The authors would like to thank Chuan Chen for providing the World Bank-PPIAF Chinese projects database, and Murong Xin and Wenxia Tang for research assistance.

21. In economics, a public good is a good that is both non-rival and non-excludable. Nonrivalry means that "each individual's consumption of such a good leads to no subtractions from any other individual's consumption of that good" (Samuelson 1954). Nonexcludability means that it is impossible to exclude any individual from consuming the good. There are, however, debates on what constitute "pure" public goods or services, and semipublic goods and services, and the appropriate roles of governments in providing, or in the case of semipublic goods, regulating them.

SIX

China Uses Its Comparative Advantage to Help Africa in Light Manufacturing

> **Box 6.1 Chapter at a glance**
>
> The emergence of Brazil, China, and India onto the global arena has created an unprecedented opportunity for other developing countries. In China, after achieving rapid and dramatic structural transformation over nearly four decades, can provide ideas, tacit knowledge, experience, and development finance and investment for transformation.
>
> As real wages rise in China and in other upper-middle-income countries, some labor-intensive light manufacturing jobs will be relocated, along with outward direct investment, to other developing countries. From historical experiences, any low-income country that captures this opportunity can have dynamic growth for several decades, generating jobs, eradicating poverty, and becoming a middle- or even a high-income country. Special economic zones and foreign direct investment have special roles to play in this.

Changes in the Comparative Advantages of the Republic of Korea and China

Chapter 4 shows that revealed comparative advantage (RCA) can measure comparative advantage in a commodity or product at any point in time, and that it will change over time. Thus it is possible to identify tradable goods that have performed well in international markets, but have begun to lose competitiveness in the comparator country. This implies that some international market space for these tradable goods may be opening up. In other words, "sunset" industries detected in a comparator country could well become "sunrise" industries elsewhere. And when such shifts take place, these comparator-country industries are likely to look to relocate to new locations that will offer continued competitive conditions, such as lower production costs, thus also providing a source of foreign direct investment (FDI) for countries interested in targeting those sectors.

Economists have used RCA analysis to explain the flying geese pattern and global industrial relocation. They find that in earlier stages of development, latecomers are likely to engage in primary product exports and labor-intensive light manufacturing. Then, as their labor cost rises, their RCA on labor-intensive light manufacturing declines.

Before World War II, Japan was a country of labor-intensive industries, with textiles and other light industrial goods accounting for 60–75 percent of its exports. But things started to change after the war. By the 1960s, at a GDP per capita about 35 percent of the United States, Japan was targeting the more capital-intensive industries moving out of America. Historical labor statistics show that a rising share of labor in Japan's manufacturing sector coincided with a declining share of labor in U.S. manufacturing. In the 1970s, Japan's RCA in labor-intensive industries such as clothing and footwear fell sharply, and its RCA in heavy manufacturing sectors was rising, notably in

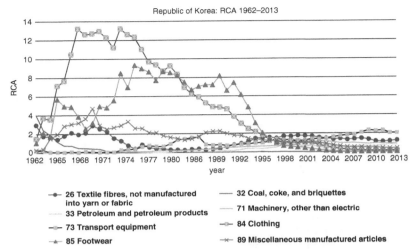

Figure 6.1 Republic of Korea's RCA: Declines in labor-intensive sectors,
1962–2013
Note: RCA = share of an industry in the economy's exports/its share in
global exports.
Source: Authors' calculation based on UN Comtrade data, SITC rev.1,
2-digit.

machinery and automobiles. In the 1980s and 1990s, just as the
United States was upgrading its industries, Japan acquired market
shares in home appliances, electronics, and computers. Similar flying
geese patterns have been observed in the Republic of Korea (Chandra
et al. 2013). Figure 6.1 shows that Korea's RCA was high in labor-
intensive sectors, clothing, footwear, and textiles from the 1960s to
the 1980s but declined after 1989, and its RCA in transportation
equipment rose after 2000.

China is now at a stage where Western countries and Japan were
in the 1970s, and the Republic Korea; Taiwan, China; and
Singapore were in the 1980s, with RCAs declining in some labor-
intensive sectors (Figure 6.2). As labor-intensive industries matured,
wages increased and firms moved into more technologically sophisticated industries in accord with the upgrading of the endowment

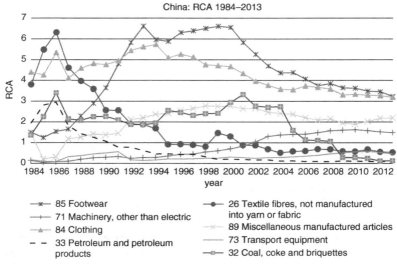

Figure 6.2 China's RCA: Declines in labor-intensive export sectors, 1982–2013

Note: RCA = share of an industry in the economy's exports/its share in global exports.

Source: Authors' calculation based on UN Comtrade data, SITC rev.1, 2-digit.

structure. China's labor costs are rising rapidly, for example, from an average of US$150 per month in 2005, to US$500 in 2012, and to more than US$600 in coastal regions in 2013 (at 15 percent annually, plus an average currency appreciation of nearly 3 percent).

More and more Chinese enterprises facing the pressure to seek low-cost locations are moving inland or going abroad. China has an estimated 124 million workers in manufacturing, most of them in labor-intensive sectors (85 million), compared with 9.7 million in Japan in 1960 and 2.3 million in the Republic of Korea in 1980. The upgrading of China's manufacturing into more sophisticated and higher value-added products and tasks will open great opportunities for labor-abundant, lower-income countries to produce the labor-intensive light-manufacturing goods that China leaves behind (Lin 2012c; Chandra et al. 2013)

Special Economic Zones or Industrial Parks

The idea that industrial parks can promote structural transformation is not new. Economists have emphasized that industrial parks or zones take advantage of dynamic scale economies and reduce search, learning, and transaction costs (Arrow 1962; Greenwald and Stiglitz 1986; Krugman 1991; Stiglitz 1996; Aoki et al. 1997; Lin and Monga 2011). The role of special economic zones (SEZs) or industrial parks has been proven by the successful experiences of emerging markets, especially among East Asian countries. In particular, investing in SEZs can

- Bundle public services in a geographically concentrated area.
- Improve the efficiency of limited government funding/budget for infrastructure.
- Facilitate cluster development or agglomeration of certain industries.
- Propel urban development by providing conducive living conditions for workers and diaspora science and technical personnel, and by conglomerating services, inducing economies of scale for environmental services.
- Stimulate job creation and income generation and, potentially, environmental sustainability through promoting green growth and ecofriendly cities (Lin and Wang 2013, p. 14).

Countries, especially those developing, cannot build business infrastructure in one go. They have few resources and low implementation capacities. They also have limited political capital to defend policies and reforms against vested interest groups and other political opposition. Such conditions require targeted interventions or piloting, especially in the initial stages.

The basic concept of a park or SEZ is simple. It is a geographically delimited area, usually physically secured. It has single management or administration. It offers benefits for investors physically within the zone. And it has a separate customs area (duty-free benefits) and streamlined procedures (World Bank 2008). In addition, a park or SEZ normally operates under more liberal economic laws than those prevailing in the country. In general, the parks or SEZs confer two main types of benefits, which in part explain their popularity: "static" economic benefits such as employment generation, export growth, government revenues and foreign exchange earnings; and more "dynamic" economic benefits such as skills upgrading, technology transfer and innovation, economic diversification, and productivity enhancement of local firms (Zeng 2010).

Despite achieving mixed results, the number of new zones has increased rapidly since the mid-1980s, with particular growth in developing countries. For example, in 1986, the International Labour Organization's database of SEZs reported 176 zones in 47 countries, and 3,500 zones in 130 countries in 2006 (Boyenge 2007). The rise of nontraditional special economic zones (SEZs), differing from export processing zones, and their success in contributing to export-led growth in East Asia are partially attributable to an era of trade and investment globalization that started in the 1980s and accelerated in the 1990s and 2000s, driven by the fragmentation of manufacturing into geographically dispersed global production networks.

Using Zones to Promote Trade and Investment

Since the 1970s, starting in East Asia and Latin America, SEZs have been designed to attract investment in labor-intensive manufacturing from multinational corporations. SEZs became a cornerstone of trade and investment policy in countries shifting away from import-substitution policies and aiming to integrate into global markets through export-led growth policies.

- China used its SEZs, particularly Shenzhen, as experimental laboratories for economic reforms that would have been politically risky to adopt nationally (Zeng 2010). Sweeping reforms were introduced through the Shenzhen SEZ, including the abolition of price controls, the introduction of the first labor contracts along with pensions and labor insurance, the privatization of state-owned enterprises, and the opening of the banking system to foreign investment. Most recently, the government is piloting full flotation of the yuan in Shenzhen. (Examples of China-supported SEZs in Africa are in Box 6.2.)

• Mauritius used its SEZ regime as a bulwark for reform over several decades, introducing labor reforms and gradually shifting the economy's focus from import substitution to export promotion (Baissac 2011). With its most recent "duty-free island" initiative, reforms once started inside the SEZs now encompass the country.

• Democratic Republic of Congo and Kenya are using recent draft SEZ legislation to incorporate provisions with a sectoral focus on areas such as mining, agriculture, and information and communications technology, which are areas of regulation not found in traditional export-oriented, light manufacturing–focused legislation for export processing zones (Zeng 2015).

Using Parks or SEZs to Spur Green and Sustainable Development

For the sustainability of park or zone programs, it is important to consider social and environmental aspects beyond economic outcomes because, over time, all these aspects intertwine. Programs that fail to offer opportunities for quality employment and upward mobility of trained staff or fail to address particular concerns of female workers are unlikely to succeed sustainably. Such programs need to emphasize social and environmental compliance issues, establishing clear standards, and implementing effective monitoring and evaluation systems. These programs can also be leveraged to promote innovative green industries. China and India are already developing guidelines and policies

Box 6.2 China-supported economic cooperation zones in Africa: Some examples

The Chinese government has backed six SEZs or industrial parks in Africa (Braütigam and Tang 2013). But many others are initiated and largely financed by the private sector, including the two discussed here. Investment in infrastructure in the zones is closely related to enterprise/cluster development in manufacturing.

An enterprise zone in Nigeria with strong local linkage. Yuemei Group, a private textile firm from China, invested in Nigeria and helped local value chain development. With its approach of "rural households plus the company," it installed over 4,000 weaving machines among local households, raising household incomes. In 2008, it invested in building a textile industrial zone. After the first phase, in 2009, it had attracted five enterprises, creating 1,000 jobs.

Ethiopia: The Eastern Industrial Park, a MOFCOM-approved zone. The Jiangsu Yongyuan Group, the founder and investor for the park, has received some funding from the China-Africa Development Fund. Since construction began in 2007, a 50,000 m² standard plant with water, roads, and power supply facilities has been completed. When we visited it in 2013, 11 Chinese enterprises with US$91 million invested had signed letters of intent to move in, in industries such as construction materials, steel products (plates and pipes), home appliances, garments, leather processing, and automobile assembly. One of the companies, the Huajian Shoemaking Group, has created over 3,500 local jobs and is using local leather to produce shoes for export. The zone now has 100 percent occupancy and has gained strong support from the government. Similar industrial parks or zones are being established elsewhere in the country.

Source: Authors.

for green zones, while many other countries (including the Republic of Korea and Thailand) are focusing on systemic development of eco-industrial parks (Yeo and Akinci 2011).

Using Parks or SEZs to Promote FDI–Local Economic Linkages

SEZs are often criticized for being "enclaves" that operate independent of the national economy. Operating outside the regulatory environment and constraints of the domestic economy is fundamental to their design and appeal, but it is also an inherent weakness since it limits multipliers, dampens prospects of technology and knowledge spillovers, and prevents FDI from becoming embedded. Important strategic and policy decisions in the early stages of SEZ program design can have significant impacts on the chances of establishing linkages to the local economy. These relate to (among other areas) the strategic/sectoral focus, encouragement of domestic firm participation, trade policy, and access to local markets (Farole et al. 2013).[1]

Chinese Investment and Entrepreneurs in Africa

Total Chinese outbound FDI in 2014 reached a peak of US$123.7 billion, but only a small share, less than 3 percent of the total, went to Africa (MOFCOM 2015). Forty-five percent of China's outward FDI was from the private sector. In many parts of Africa, a wide range of Chinese businesses – manufacturers of garments, shoes, leather goods, and food producers – have become an everyday sight (Shen 2015).

Based on home country data, "Private Chinese firms have become aggressive in Africa in recent years, [and] their accumulated project number increased from 52 in 2005 to 1,217 in 2013, representing 53 percent of all Chinese [outward] FDI projects currently in the continent" (Shen 2015, p. 87) "There is a stark contrast between private and government investment in terms of sectors. The former

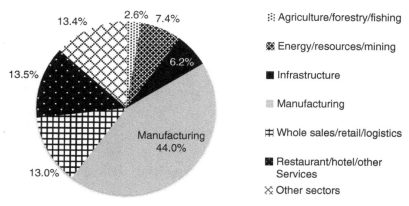

Figure 6.3 Chinese investment in six African countries: Nigeria, Ethiopia, Zambia, Ghana, Liberia, and Rwanda
Note: Using host government data
Source: Shen 2015.

is overwhelmingly concentrated in manufacturing and services, with the latter in construction and mining" (Shen 2015, p. 88).

Shen found, however, that:

- Based on host government data, MOFCOM statistics greatly underestimate China's total outward FDI, by around 3 to 1.
- The private sector – usually small to midsized privately held firms – is responsible for 55 percent of Chinese FDI in Africa.
- Manufacturing accounts for the bulk of private Chinese investment. Based on host country data, Chinese private investment is heavily concentrated in labor-intensive manufacturing, accounting for 44 percent of the number of projects in six countries, followed by service industries (Figure 6.3)
- Chinese investment produces jobs. African leaders appreciate them but express concern about the paucity of "technology transfer" and "language and cultural barriers" (Shen 2015).

Shen also found that Chinese firms come to Africa because their domestic market is saturated and African labor costs are less than

Chinese labor, even though operating in Africa is expensive due to infrastructure gaps and security issues (Shen 2015).

Chinese Engagement in Ethiopia's Leather Processing Value Chain[2]

From 2010 to 2015, leather processing and leather product manufacturing in Ethiopia received growing investment from China. Chinese investors set up large tanneries (to process leather), and new shoe and glove factories relocated from China, substantially boosting Ethiopia's manufacturing. At the start, tanneries and manufacturers had little mutual interaction, and their impacts on the local economy seemed to diverge, too. But it seems likely that they will complement each other and contribute to developing the entire leather-processing value chain in the long run.

Ethiopia is believed to have the second largest livestock population in Africa. Ethiopian sheepskin is famous for its quality and has high demand in international markets. China was an increasingly important export market for the country's leather, rising from 2 percent of leather exports in 2000 to 31 percent in 2010 (UN Comtrade Statistics 2015). But facing steep competition for high-quality Ethiopian skins, five Chinese leather firms set up tanneries in Ethiopia to secure supplies. Three other leather-products firms (two Indian and one British) also invested in the country.

Initially, all the processed leather of the Chinese tanneries was exported, mainly to China, encouraged by the Ethiopian government, which was eager to earn foreign exchange. The importance of China as a market continued growing, to account for nearly 58 percent of Ethiopia's leather exports in 2013 (UN Comtrade Statistics 2015). In addition, a Chinese tannery, Koka Addis, began to supply leather to the Chinese Huajian Shoemaking Group, which had established a factory in Ethiopia.

Since their primary interest was in acquiring raw materials, foreign tanneries originally planned to export semi-processed leather (wet blue) or unfinished leather (crust). But the government changed policies in 2008 and again in 2011, imposing a 150 percent export tax, first on wet blue and then on crust, prompting all tanneries in Ethiopia to upgrade their machinery. The China-Africa Overseas Tannery, of which China Africa Development Fund is a shareholder, spent nearly RMB 200 million (US$33 million) buying advanced processing equipment and claimed to be the number one firm in Ethiopia for varieties of processed leather.

Some Chinese investors were reluctant, however, to move into finished leather exports. They explained that part of the leather they exported would normally be further processed by firms at home in response to market demand. Finishing the leather in Ethiopia raised their costs and reduced product appeal to their clients, who followed the latest fashion and needed quick responses and new designs; the style and color of Ethiopian-finished leather might have jeopardized that market-response time. As one tannery owner said, "Risks are high because it is not connected to the market. It takes too long for finished leather to catch up with the market. And the color and style of skins do not always match. For example, there are many shades of brown. A small difference between skins can make it unsalable. Finished products need to allow clients to connect flexibly with markets."[3] The quality of leather finished in Ethiopia was also said to be low due to underdeveloped facilities, skills, and chemical supplies.

Interaction between Chinese and Ethiopian tanneries was scarce. A few local tanneries had negative views of Chinese investors, believing that they were mainly interested in securing Ethiopian raw materials, not adding value locally, and that they had driven up prices. In their view, the Chinese and other foreign tanneries had not brought truly advanced processing technologies to Ethiopia. By comparison, Chinese tanneries considered themselves stronger in having market connections and understanding clients' demands, but thought that local tanneries had better access to raw skins.

Simultaneously but independently, Chinese firms engaged in Ethiopia's leather product manufacturing. By January 2015, three medium to large firms from Greater China (including Hong Kong, China and Taiwan, China) had set up production bases in the country. The largest one, Huajian Shoemaking Group, a major shoe company in southern China, had invested US$30 million and hired 3,400 workers, of whom 96.5 percent were Ethiopian. The other two firms had hired 1,000 and 800 people each. A British and German firm also relocated its Chinese glove factories to Ethiopia, both bringing in Chinese technicians to train Ethiopian workers.

Chinese manufacturers were attracted to Ethiopia mainly by cheap labor, given that labor costs had been rising steeply in China. Some also viewed the abundant supplies of leather as an advantage. Huajian had 24,000 workers in China in 2011. The average monthly wage was RMB 2,000–3,000 (US$300–450), while Ethiopian workers earned as little as 600 Birr (US$35) a month. The president of Huajian had visited Ethiopia for the first time in October 2011. A mere three months later, the group opened a factory with 600 workers in the Chinese-run Eastern Industrial Zone. New Wing, a Hong Kong firm that had two shoe factories in Mainland China, bought a factory in Ethiopia in May 2011 and began operations in September 2011.

Training of workers is critical for the success of these labor-intensive manufacturers. Huajian has an ambitious training program. Between 2011 and 2015, Huajian sent three groups of around 100 Ethiopian workers to China for training that lasted from three months to one year. The other foreign shoe and glove factories brought in four to 60 Chinese technicians to train local workers. Ethiopian workers took over most production after two or three years, but Chinese technicians were still required for sophisticated tasks and quality control. Since the factories in Ethiopia cannot guarantee consistent quality, however, all the firms plan to keep their factories in China to make high-end products. Their Ethiopian factories will make low- and middle-end products.

Exporting 100 percent of their products to the United States and Europe, the Chinese shoemakers were viewed positively by many Ethiopians. Local shoemakers, for example, were impressed by the immense production scale of Chinese factories. An Ethiopian factory manager recalled: "When I visited Huajian, I saw their massive operation, I was shocked. It was an army of people. Everybody was *chikchikking* (sewing and working), that's crazy!!! Ethiopians were not used to that. We could not do that. It was the first time that we saw this."[4]

In 2012, Huajian's managing director expected to break even at the end of the year. Mr. Zhang Ronghua, owner of Huajian, stated that his Ethiopian factory achieved the break-even point in 2012 and made more than 10 percent profit in 2013.[5] (New Wing was running at less than 40 percent of capacity because of transport and logistics bottlenecks.) He intended to shift more production capacity to Ethiopia. "Our factories in Dongguan China were producing 10,000 pairs a day, now only 5,000 a day, we hope that in the future we can do 1,000 pairs a day, because the price (for the workers) is crazy." He said that many U.S. and European customers still do not accept shoes made in Africa, but "when they accept, we are ready."[6]

Most of these manufacturers extended to upstream supplies. New Wing has established its own tannery and produces soles and shoe boxes in Ethiopia. Newly arrived George Co. – a Taiwan, China, shoemaker – also plans to build a tannery. British glove manufacturer Pittards has its own tannery to supply all leather demanded. For the leather-product companies, moving upstream is partly caused by deficient local supply. As New Wing's manager said, "No (local) tannery can produce as many kinds of leather as we need."[7] Huajian built a factory to produce soles and other shoe materials; it sourced 100 percent of its leather supply from Ethiopian tanneries in 2014. A tannery owned by Koka Addis recently became one of its suppliers. The owner of Koka Addis is confident that he will win the competition against local tanneries: "We are better at providing

service, we can control color differences and quality instability ...
Huajian has urged me to get machines to supply more for them."[8]

For Huajian, the company's success seems attributable to:

- Strong support and commitment by Ethiopian's top leadership in enhancing investor confidence in the government's willingness to help reduce transaction costs.
- Local value chains and supporting industries developed with assistance from donors and UN specialized agencies, such as UNIDO.
- Attracting one of China's labor-intensive sectors being priced out of China.
- Using the comparative advantage of high-quality leather and inexpensive labor in Ethiopia.
- Following an original equipment manufacturer approach that facilitates learning, tacit knowledge transfer, and capacity development. It has also taken advantage of trade agreements, such as the African Growth and Opportunity Act in the United States and the Everything but Arms initiative in the European Union.

In conclusion, a handful of large Chinese investments in Ethiopia's leather processing and manufacturing sectors have greatly transformed the structure and modus operandi of local industries. They have brought capital, technology, tacit knowledge, management skills, and market connections to the country. While individual firms face obstacles, the arrival of international upstream and downstream firms may help solve critical bottlenecks along the supply chain. And policies to encourage local vertical linkages may attract more Chinese investors to relocate their production to Ethiopia.

Chinese Investments in the Textile and Apparel Sector in Sub-Saharan Africa[9]

Under the flying geese model, economists expect the textile and apparel sector to boost industrialization in Africa. Chinese companies' engagements in this sector in Africa are thus particularly interesting, as they are the world's major players and have the potential to help shape the continent's industrialization.

Chinese investors in garment making have focused on South Africa, Lesotho, Swaziland, and Botswana. Some were originally from Taiwan, China; their business in the region started as early as the 1970s. These companies from Taiwan, China, recruited technicians from Greater China, and many of those technicians later opened their own factories. As the Chinese economy grew, more and more investors from Greater China came to southern Africa, usually forming clusters to share information, build connections, and seek business. In the more established clusters, they found machinery sales agents and expatriate technicians of Chinese origin.

Chinese producers in Southern Africa used to export garments to the European and U.S. markets when African governments offered generous financial incentives to encourage foreign investments in export businesses. But as the tax holidays ended, most Chinese firms left the export business. As with the Ethiopia case, the main reason was that clients in those two markets have strict requirements on quality and lead time, which African factories were unable to guarantee, and some manufacturers even had to pay huge penalties for infractions. Other issues – such as increasing labor conflicts, deficient facilities, a cumbersome export process, and a lack of local industrial suppliers – greatly raised transaction costs and left their factories unable to compete with those based in China and other Asian countries.

Most Chinese garment producers still in Africa sell their products almost exclusively to the South African market. A fast-fashion business model has been adopted by major retailers in South Africa, requiring one-week responses to changes in fashion. Local suppliers have the advantage of short lead times against Asian imports and can survive in this niche market. Hundreds of private investors from China and Taiwan, China, are operating cut, make, and trim

(CMT) or cut, make, and pack (CMP) factories. They are all small, on average about 100–200 people, and require little capital (as little as US$20,000) to start. They can easily relocate to places where production costs are lower.

Yet China JD Group, a giant apparel maker, set up a long-term production base in Tanzania in 2011. Its motives were different. In 2005, feeling pressure from rising production costs, it set up factories in Cambodia, where it now has 13 plants, employing more than 20,000 workers. But average wages there have been rising from US$40 per month to US$150. So the company, with its clients in the United States (its main market), began to search for a new production site.

It came to Tanzania through an old aid project, Urafiki Textile Co. in Dar es Salaam. Tanzania's stable political situation, good relations with China, and a new SEZ helped the CEO make up his mind. Within a year of his first visit in May 2011, the group opened its first factory in Dar es Salaam. By August 2014, it had hired 1,300 local workers. A second factory was to be completed in October 2015 with 2,500 local workers. All products are exported to the U.S. market.

The first factory served rather as an experiment. This experience would soon be used to set up many more factories, just as the group got a foothold in Cambodia before expanding. "When we establish a factory with tens of thousands of employees, it cannot be a short-term investment. We want to stay at least 20 to 30 years," said Wang Wenping of the group's Tanzania branch.[10]

A main bottleneck facing all Chinese apparel makers in Africa is the supply of fabrics and accessories, so most are imported from China, raising costs and operational difficulties and causing production delays. Only a few textile mills in sub-Saharan Africa produce fabric for apparel but do not achieve scale economies. Chinese factories in China, in contrast, run the complete value chain of textile and apparel production. With a vast number of mills and many accessory suppliers, they can supply the amounts and varieties garment makers require, at good prices.

Seeing the gap, several companies from China and Taiwan China set up textile mills in Africa, including Urafiki in Tanzania and Taiyuan in South Africa. Yet their performance is unsatisfactory, mainly due to low local worker productivity and unstable power supplies. "If we had done a better investigation, we would not have invested here," the CEO of Taiyuan said, expressing regret over the venture.[11] China JD Group has plans to extend to weaving and dyeing in Tanzania in a few years, as the firm's operations in China cover textile processing. But Wang is cautious. "A textile mill needs a lot of equipment. The investment amount is big. We are not in hurry to unfold all the plans immediately. We should do it step by step."[12]

In 2013 and 2014, a small Chinese textile and apparel cluster emerged in Ethiopia, as three textile mills and one garment maker set up in a Chinese-run industrial park. Yet they did not coordinate with each other, making almost simultaneous investments coincidentally. Rising wages and environmental standards in China pushed the textile manufacturers to seek cheaper manufacturing space overseas, and the Ethiopian government's support and incentives attracted them.

These companies target mainly the Ethiopian and regional East African markets. All of them produce only polyester cloth and garments, which are technically less demanding to make and more affordable to African consumers. Since the start of operations, sales have been very promising, but the firms found many unexpected problems on the production side: delays in customs clearance, frequent leaves of local workers, unprofessional service providers. The owner of one mill summarized his experience in Ethiopia: "As long as people can make the products, they can make money."[13]

Scattered Chinese textile and apparel investments can also be found elsewhere in Africa, often driven by China's industrial upgrading. Yet not all African countries will benefit from relocation. Chinese investors will be attracted only to countries with government commitments to provide investors with a reasonable business environment. Access to domestic and international markets, functioning infrastructure, political stability, financial incentives, and other elements will influence Chinese investors' choice of destination. In addition, governments need to do more to strengthen foreign factories' linkage with local supplies, for them to expand and stay longer in Africa.

Notes

1. The Masan Free Trade Zone in the Republic of Korea offers a successful example of promoting zone–local economic linkages.
2. This section contributed by Tang Xiaoyang, Deborah Braütigam, and Margaret McMillan, based on field research during 2012–2015, and supported by a grant of the Private Enterprise Development in Low-Income Countries (PEDL).
3. Interview, Zhang Jianxin, owner of Koka Addis tannery, Modjo, January 2015.
4. Interview, Girma Ayalew, Deputy Manager Fontanina, Addis, February 2015.
5. Private conversation with Justin Yifu Lin.
6. Interview, Renzo Bertini, Manager of New Wing Shoe Factory, January 2015.
7. Ibid.
8. Interview, Zhang Jianxin, January 2015.
9. Based on Tang Xiaoyang: "The Impact of Asian Investment on Africa's Textile Industries," Carnegie-Tsinghua Center for Global Policy Paper, Beijing, China, August 2014, with updates drawing on interviews.
10. Interview, Wang Wenping, China JD Group, Tanzania branch, Dar es Salaam, August 2013.
11. Interview, CEO of Taiyuan Textile Mill, Ladysmith, South Africa, July 2013.
12. Interview, Wang Wenping, August 2013.
13. Interview, owner of Kaipu Spinning, Dukem, Ethiopia, January 2015.

SEVEN

Effectiveness for Transformation: The Secret for Quick Wins

Box 7.1 Chapter at a glance

Development is a complex process full of uncertainty and risks. This chapter discusses development effectiveness by asking "What is effectiveness?" and "Effectiveness for what"?

Southern providers of aid are also facing a steep learning curve: They suffer from the lack of theorizing their development ideas, the lack of clarity on philosophies underlying their provision of aid, the absence of laws and regulations on foreign aid, and the lack of transparency in the terms and conditions related to aid and investment.

When discussing aid effectiveness, we must ask, "effective for what"? Even though both North and South partners held several international conferences on aid effectiveness, there is still an imbalance on whether voices from Southern partners are heard. Candid discussions and exchanges of ideas about the shortcomings or ineffectiveness of each approach can indeed promote mutual learning and understanding. From the angle of structural transformation, the most effective way to jump-start

---

> **Box 7.1** (*Cont.*)
>
> a low-income economy is to target the sectors that the country may have latent comparative advantage and to use the "advantage of backwardness" by attracting outward FDI from successful emerging economies. The Growth Identification and Facilitation (GIF) framework describes innovative ways to target and achieve "quick wins," and such quick wins are effective for economic transformation.

African heads of state and policymakers have highlighted the importance of China's engagement in Africa, including providing Africans with new ideas, an alternative "model," and new leverage in relation to other donors. They welcome China's continuing support for Africa's development, noting that China's trade and investment has contributed to Africa's growth. And they appreciate China's principle of mutual respect and noninterference in domestic affairs, and its focus on infrastructure and direct investment in manufacturing, thus removing bottlenecks and building capacity for longer-term growth.[1]

African officials also welcome Chinese engagement in African infrastructure development, both as an example of good practice and a source of financing and capacity building. But they also express frustration over a lack of transparency in the terms of government-sponsored commercial deals and in China's development cooperation activities, demanding more predictability and stability of aid and more donor coordination. For African countries to be fully in the driver's seat in their relations with China and other emerging donors, they need more complete information on the levels and conditions of assistance. Development partners, especially emerging market partners, thus need to be more forthcoming about their aid programs, including experiences and lessons learned from the many years of engagement in Africa, to avoid repeating past mistakes.

The Forum of China and Africa Cooperation (FOCAC), held six times since 2000 and in 2015 in South Africa, has been striving to achieve precisely this. On December 4 and 5, Chinese President Xi Jinping spoke at the sixth forum in Johannesburg, South Africa, and proposed 10 major plans for African development, including structural transformation, industrial upgrading, South-South learning, and capacity development. He also referred to an investment commitment of US$60 billion in three years (a tripling from 2012) including US$5 billion for grants and interest-free loans, US$35 billion for concessional loans and export buyers' credit, and the rest for commercial financing (Annex 7.1). These proposals were warmly welcomed by African leaders and friends. How, then, to overcome some weaknesses in China's South-South Development Cooperation and improve development effectiveness?

Four Steps for Improving China's South-South Development Cooperation

China faces a steep learning curve for international development cooperation. African policymakers cite the absence of a foreign aid law and legislation on decision-making; the lack of an independent aid administration; the inadequate coordination across ministries and agencies; the lack of transparency; and the uneven capacity among China's providers of cooperation, aid, and investment. This is not just China, of course. Greater exchanges of ideas between established and emerging providers of aid and cooperation would benefit both sides.

A first challenge is a lack of transparency in China's South-South Development Cooperation projects: official project data are hard to get. The publication of the White Paper on China's Foreign Aid (State Council 2011 and 2014) and a series of publications on China Africa Economic and Trade Cooperation (MOFCOM 2013 and other years) are steps in the right direction. But the government needs to be yet more open and proactive in providing better data, and making laws and regulations clear. This would also increase the government's accountability to taxpayers in China and to the international development community.

Since China does not have a legal framework for foreign aid and has no independent aid agency, it is hard for its citizens to take part in decisions on foreign aid, for Chinese officials to be held accountable, and for international bodies and governments to collaborate on international development or financing issues. In our view, a law on foreign aid and cooperation and the establishment of an independent aid agency should be priorities. The Asian Infrastructure Investment Bank (AIIB) and the New Development Bank may pressure the authorities to think about not only governing these institutions but also reviewing overall legitimacy and governance of foreign aid and cooperation under law.

A second concern is "tied aid" and inadequate technological diffusion and spillover effects. At least half of Chinese aid is tied to goods and services provided by Chinese companies, a practice the members of OECD–DAC agreed to move away from progressively since 1995. (Tied aid can increase costs and reduce efficiency.)[2] But China's experience indicates that tied aid has some advantages for facilitating learning-by-doing and learning by implementing projects. In the 1980s and 1990s, most bilateral donor-financed projects in China were tied aid, yet Chinese workers and project managers learned and benefited from them (Wang 2011a). Actually, "learning from implementing aid projects" is one of the reasons Chinese companies are so competitive in construction projects.

The new development banks will, according to their articles of agreement, implement the highest international standards for competitive bidding, procurement, and social and environmental standards. Their corporate governance will serve as an example and a "pressure mechanism" for all banks, funds, institutional investors, and companies from China and other emerging markets. In this sense, international competition is good for aid effectiveness.

We propose that some China financed projects to have international or local competitive bidding, especially in small components of a larger projects, in order to benefit local SMEs in construction and manufacturing business. Host governments can also have such regulations that x percent of subcomponents should be subject to local competitive bidding.

A third concern is that Chinese aid and cooperation projects seem to have generated few local jobs. Many African officials are concerned that Chinese workers are displacing local workers. Although data need to be discussed case by case, indirect employment generation from China-financed economic infrastructure has been under-researched.[3]

A fourth concern is about labor and environmental standards and the practices of Chinese companies. Some Chinese companies have yet to fully comply with domestic laws and regulations, for which they need more education and training. These companies should also be reviewed and evaluated by host governments. Here the role of local government regulators, parliamentarians, nongovernmental organizations, media, and civil society, as well as the international community is important to induce desired partner behavior and, if necessary, to sanction offenders. The Chinese government should listen to the voices of development partners more attentively, encouraging firms to fulfill their corporate social responsibilities and to work closely with the local community and civil society organization. One significant part of the learning is to have a better results framework for development projects, better social and environmental safeguards, and better monitor and evaluation systems.

We propose establishing an international system for rating and ranking the behaviors of all partners and companies in the development arena, using criteria consistent with inclusive and sustainable structural transformation. The rating or ranking criteria should cover quantity, quality, relevance, and efficacy as well as efficiency, inclusiveness, and sustainability. Partners and companies implementing projects with the following characteristics should, in our view, be given higher scores:

- Projects that release bottlenecks and facilitate the cluster development and agglomeration of various industries and services.
- Projects associated with renewable energy, green-technology and eco-industrial parks; banks practicing green financing principles, including but not limited to the Equator principles; companies following the Extractive Industries Transparency Initiative principles of the transparency.
- Infrastructure projects in and around eco-industrial parks and special economic zones are especially transformative because they can help "bundling public services" in a geographically concentrated area, reduce transaction costs, and facilitate cluster development and scale economies. They can also facilitate urbanization and industrial relocation and upgrading.

Under such a clear system of indicators for monitoring and evaluation, all partners and companies would try their best to compete with others. This would help align the incentive structures for inclusive and sustainable development, fully consistent with the Sustainable Development Goals for 2030.

No two countries are the same in their economic transformation. China has made some mistakes and paid high tuition fees in the process, such as widening rural–urban income disparities and a degraded environment. In March 2007, former Chinese Premier Wen Jiabao said, "Chinese economy was unstable, unbalanced, uncoordinated and unsustainable."[4] Since then, there have been efforts to rebalance the economy – paying more attention to the quality of growth and to environmental sustainability. Yet making deep transformations and upgrading industry is extremely difficult.

African countries need to be selective to avoid the mistakes China made. African governments, NGOs, and civil society can push China and Chinese companies, as well as other development partners, in the right direction. Establishing the proposed monitoring, evaluation, and ranking system would help discipline the partners' behaviors.

China's Alternative Approach for Growth and Development

An ideal development partnership should be based on the "diversity and complementarity" of policy ideas (I. Ohno, JICA). [5] We agree. If all donor advice is the same, how can partner countries choose and combine ideas? How can they be empowered with new ideas? Therefore, a new type of partnership should be more tolerant of alternative ideas and approaches so that partner countries can select and combine these ideas.

How do ideas differ between the China's approach of development and approach in South-South cooperation? As discussed in Chapters 3 and 4, Chinese leaders approach the complex problems of development with humility, using a learning and experimenting approach, acknowledging what we know and what we do not know.

Using a joint learning approach, Africa and China are all learners on equal footing: Africans have some comparative advantages, and China has different comparative advantages. In the process of climbing the same mountain of structural transformation, Africa and China can complement each other and reach win-win solutions. But China's South-South Development Cooperation, based on the New Structural Economics, provides new ideas for ways to climb up the industrial upgrading ladder.

China has been widely regarded as an alternative model in Africa, differing from the Washington Consensus and market fundamentalism, or "neo-liberalism" as it is called by Ostry et al. (2016) of the

IMF. This has allowed African policymakers to have a choice, giving them leverage in negotiations with other partners. Part of the model is support for Africa's infrastructure development, including roads, bridges, hydropower, and other power generation and transmission services, which has helped alleviate Africa's many infrastructure bottlenecks (Chapter 5). Another is China's support for special economic zones (SEZs) and industrial parks, promoting the agglomeration of manufacturing (Chapter 6). A third is targeting sectors with latent comparative advantage, which we now turn to.

Development Ideas Missing in North-South Aid: Targeting as Industrial Policy for Structural Transformation

OECD countries have used many industrial policies to target the sectors they wanted to develop, and developing countries can learn from these experiences (Chang 2003). Mariana Mazzucato reviewed the experiences of United Kingdom and the United States on industrial policies, and found that the state "has not just fixed markets, but actively created them" (2011, p. 1). She described many industrial policies that the United States has used to support Internet development, green-energy technology, the pharmaceutical sector, and defense and air and space programs.[6] Joseph Stiglitz points out that "all countries utilize industrial policies but some simply do not know it," giving examples of U.S. industrial policy through bailing out the automobile and financial sectors.[7] Ha-Joon Chang has been "at the forefront of arguing in the context of historical paths to development, those that have traversed it insist, 'Do not do as we did, do as we say'" (quote from Fine 2011, p. 3).

Many countries have targeted industrial sectors as priorities for attracting FDI, according to Alfaro and Charlton (2014), who used industry level data from 29 OECD industrial countries for 1985–2000. Ten to 12 countries targeted computers and televisions, vehicles and transport equipment, real estate and business, and

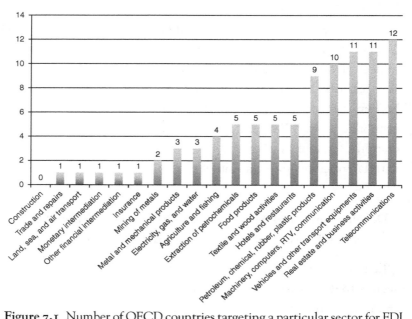

Figure 7.1 Number of OECD countries targeting a particular sector for FDI
Source: Based on data from Alfaro and Charlton 2014.

telecommunications; nine countries targeted petrochemical, rubber, and plastic products (Figure 7.1).

Developing and developed economies alike use a range of industrial policy instruments, including "targeting" and "picking winners." These tools can be broadly classified into one of eight categories: fiscal incentives; investment attraction programs; training and capacity development; infrastructure support; trade measures; public procurement; financial mechanisms; and industrial restructuring schemes (Felipe 2015; Stiglitz and Lin 2013)

Western aid programs, however, did not – and will not – tell developing countries how to use industrial policy and climb up the technology ladder, because industrial policy has been taboo in many multilateral and bilateral development institutions. SEZs and industrial parks have been missing in those aid programs as well, with a few exceptions (such as UNIDO and IFC programs). Only recently did the World Bank approve its first project for SEZs in Ethiopia, even though they had been proven successful in many East Asian countries for years. Western aid programs focus often on "what a developing country does not have," such as good governance, solid institutions, and adequate human capital. But they often ignore what a country possesses (its revealed comparative advantages) and what it could potentially do well (its latent comparative advantages).

Many developing countries are labor, land, and resource abundant and are producers of primary products in the first stage of their development. To upgrade their industrial structure, they must first facilitate the growth of sectors that they can do well in based on what they have and gradually close their endowment gaps, including physical, human, and institutional (intangible) capital, with advanced industrial nations. Consistent with the New Structural Economics (NSE), these countries ought to follow their comparative advantage, although this does not mean that they should specialize only in what they used to produce (primary products). Instead, their strategy should also be to identify what they could potentially do well; that is, to identify their latent comparative advantage. But how?

The Growth Identification and Facilitation Framework

Lin's New Structural Economics approach has generated interest in the world development community, especially in deindustrializing countries. Many prominent economists and development specialists have contributed their inputs to the NSE framework development since 2011 (Lin 2012d). This new development thinking is also gaining traction among government policymakers in the developing world. However, economists stridently debate whether targeting sectors or picking winners is a good idea for developing countries facing the challenges of weak institutional capacity and poor governance. As one scholar cautions, "[t]he first problem for the government in carrying out an industrial policy is that we actually know precious little about identifying a 'winning' industrial structure. There is not a set of economic criteria that determine what gives different countries pre-eminence in particular lines of business" (Schultze 1983).

In recent years, several economists have tried to solve the issue of identifying sectors for a country, with only limited success:

- The "growth diagnostic framework" suggested by Hausmann et al. (2005) focuses on binding constraints instead of a whole set of first-best institutions. But it relies on surveys of existing firms, which may be in a "wrong" sector as a result of "wrong" interventions in the past, and no firm would exist in the new industries where the country may have latent comparative advantage either.
- The "product space" suggested by Hausmann and Klinger (2006), Hidalgo et al. (2007) is based on the fact that *firms in existing sectors* own tacit knowledge helpful for successful upgrading in the product space. But some sectors where the country may have latent comparative advantage may be totally new to the country as well. Moreover, tacit knowledge can be "imported" and transmitted through training and learning from workers in the foreign invested enterprises.

Lin and his colleague, by contrast, consider that identifying the right target for a country (or countries) to follow, and their industries with good potential for growth and competitiveness, is a precondition for successful catch-up (Lin and Monga 2011). Why?

First, developing countries in general have poor hard and soft infrastructure, and governments always have limited resources to invest in hard and soft infrastructure, which are often sector specific. A developing country cannot be successful in all sectors. Indeed, success is often found in individual sectors, such as textiles in Mauritius, apparel in Lesotho, cut flowers in Ethiopia, or gorilla tourism in Rwanda. For cut flowers, airport refrigeration facilities and regular flights are required to ship them to markets overseas, which are obviously different from the port facilities for Mauritius's textile exports. A government must therefore choose which infrastructure elements to improve and where to provide these services to facilitate private sector activities.

Second, identification is needed because industrial clustering is essential for economies of scale and reducing costs. Specialization, agglomeration, and clustering are vital for reducing transaction costs in any given industry. The government needs to provide infrastructure services in certain locations – or incentives for first movers in certain sectors. Otherwise private firms may be spread too thinly over too many sectors, reducing the chances of these firms surviving and gaining a competitive edge in international markets.

There are many examples of failures and successes in picking winners. Ireland has both. In the 1950s, it adopted an industrial policy called a "heavy state interventionist but hands-off approach," providing tax incentives, grants, and subsidies to encourage investments that targeted exports. But there were few takers, and Ireland remained among Western Europe's poorest countries. With large outmigration, Irish were nicknamed "beggars of Europe." In the 1980s, Ireland's Investment Development Authority started to pick winners – focusing on electronics, pharmaceuticals, software, and chemicals. It courted FDI in these industries from Germany, the United Kingdom, and the United States, attracting nine of the world's top 10 pharmaceutical firms and 12 of the world's top 15 medical products companies. In addition to information and communications technology companies, leading e-business firms set up facilities in Ireland: among them, Google, Yahoo, eBay, and Amazon. The "Celtic tiger" became one of the most attractive destinations for migration from Eastern Europe (Lin 2012b).

How best to identify the right target countries and the right target industries? Lin and Monga (2011) provide the following six-step process.

Step 1: Choose the right target country. Policymakers should select dynamically growing countries with similar endowment structures and those with about 100 percent higher per capita incomes measured in purchasing power parity or those with similar per capita incomes 20 years ago. They should then identify tradable goods and services that have grown well in those countries for the past 15–20 years. These are likely to be new industries consistent with latent comparative advantage in their own countries, since countries with similar endowments are likely to have similar comparative advantage. A fast-growing country that has produced certain goods and services for about 20 years will begin to lose its comparative advantage as wages rise, leaving space for countries with lower wages to enter those industries.

Step 2: Assist domestic private firms. If some private domestic firms are already in those industries, they possess tacit knowledge necessary for those industries (Hausmann 2013). Policymakers should identify obstacles preventing these firms from upgrading their products and barriers that limit entry to those industries by other private firms. Policies can then be implemented to remove the constraints and facilitate entry.

Step 3: Attract global investors. For industries with no domestic firms present or only a small number of firms doing exports, policymakers should try to attract FDI from countries listed in the first step or from other higher income countries producing those goods. Such foreign investors may well possess the general and tacit knowledge for certain products in their design, production technology, and supply chain and distribution channels. Governments should also set up incubation programs to encourage start-ups in these industries.

Step 4: Scale-up self-discoveries. In addition to the industries identified in the first step, governments should pay attention to spontaneous self-discovery by private enterprises and support the scaling up of successful private innovation in new industries. Due to its unique endowment, a country may have some products that are valuable in international markets or that present new opportunities because of rapid technological changes arise. Examples include mobile phones and related e-services, social media, and green technologies.

Step 5: Recognize the power of industrial parks. In countries with poor infrastructure and an unfriendly business environment, the government can set up SEZs or industrial parks to help overcome barriers to firm entry and foreign investment. These zones create preferential business environments that most governments, constrained by low budgets and low capacity, are unable to quickly implement economy-wide. Establishing industrial parks or zones can also facilitate the formation of industrial clusters, reducing production and transaction costs and promoting sustainable and green industrialization.

Step 6: Provide limited incentives to the right industries. Policymakers can compensate pioneer firms in the industries identified earlier with time-limited tax incentives, cofinancing for investments, and providing access to foreign exchange. This compensates for the externalities that first movers create and encourages firms to form clusters. Because the identified industries are consistent with the country's latent comparative advantage, the firms should be viable in open, competitive markets, and the incentives should be limited in both time and financial cost. To prevent rent seeking and political capture, governments should avoid high tariffs, incentives that create monopoly rents, or other distortions. And incentives should be linked to performance and be continuously evaluated against stated objectives (Lin 2012e).

Several African countries are now attempting to follow the GIF approach to target certain countries and sectors in which they have a latent comparative advantage. (See UNIDO 2015[8] and forthcoming reports on Senegal and Ethiopia, using the GIF approach.)

In sum, with a focus on structural transformation, South-South Development Cooperation provides not only financing but also

ANNEX TABLE 7.1 *Forums and commitments on cooperation with Africa*

Africa's partnerships	Year of creation and frequency	Highest number of participation at head of state level from Africa	Major announcements at the most recent event
Forum on China-Africa Cooperation (FOCAC)	2000–2015 Triennial	45 heads of state and government (2015)	China committed to support Africa by an investment of US$60 billion (a tripling of commitments in 2012) in the next three years, including US$5 billion for grants and no-interest loans, US$35 billion for concessional loans and export buyers' credit, and the rest as commercial financing
Tokyo International Conference on African Development (TICAD)	1993 Every 5 years	41 heads of state (2008)	Contribute to the growth of Africa with private and public means of up to US$32 billion in the next five years
US-Africa Leaders' Summit	2014	45 heads of state and government (2014)	US$7 billion financing to promote American exports to and investment in Africa; US$14 billion private sector investment in clean energy, aviation, banking and construction; US$12 billion Power Africa Initiative

France-Africa Summit	1973	Annual until 1990; now biennial	Around 40 heads of state and government (2013)	Double trade with Africa in the next five years; donations and projects to reach €20 billion (about US$21 billion) in the next five years
India-Africa Forum Summit	2008, 2011, 2015		41 heads of state and government (2015)	US$10 billion concessional credit over the next five years; US$600 million grant assistance, including US$100 million India-Africa Development Fund and US$100 million India-Africa Health Fund; 50,000 scholarships over the next five years
Africa-Turkey Cooperation Summit	2008, 2014		7 presidents (2014)	Tariff-preferences and duty-free privileges to expand trade and investment from US$30 billion in 2013 to US$50 billion by 2019
Korea-Africa Forum; Forum on Economic Cooperation; Forum on Industry Cooperation	KAF: 2006, triennial KOAFEC: 2006, biennial KOAFIC: 2008, annual		5 heads of state (2006)	Increase official development assistance to Africa; expand scholarship programs for African students

Source: South-South Policy Team at UNDP. Issue Brief No. 14, December 2015.

development theories and ideas, using such methods as the GIF approach to identify target countries and target industries and to help host partner countries in industrial upgrading. That is, it helps identify growth pillars in low-income countries and eases the joint effort to "climb up the mountain of structural transformation together" to achieve win-win solutions.

Notes

1. Some commentators have also suggested that China's approach "engenders ownership and self-reliance" (Manji 2009, p. 7).
2. See, for example, Morrisey and White 1996.
3. See, for example, Weisbrod and Whalley 2011.
4. See Chinese former Premier Wen Jiabao's March 16, 2007, speech in a press conference: http://news.xinhuanet.com/english/2007-03/16/content_5856569 .htm.
5. Comments made by Izumi Ohno during a conference organized by China-OECD/DAC Study Group (for which Yan Wang was a coordinator), October 2009, Beijing.
6. Mazzucato 2011.
7. Speech at the UNIDO 50th Anniversary Conference, December 5, 2015.
8. UNIDO and Peking University, Technical Note on the analytical framework of GIFIUD. Available at https://isid.unido.org/files/Senegal/final-technical-note-on-the-analytical-framework-of-gifiud.pdf.

EIGHT

Prospects for Development Finance

One who wishes himself to be successful must also help others to be successful; one who wishes to develop himself also hopes to help others develop.

（"己欲立而立人,己欲达而达人"）.

Confucius, *Lunyu-Yongye*, circa 475–221 B.C.

Be independent and strive for the better when you are poor; help and benefit the others when you are rich.

"穷则独善其身 , 达则兼济天下" 出自《孟子》的《尽心章句上》。

Mencius, in his book *Menzi*, circa 372–289 BC

Box 8.1 Chapter at a glance

This concluding chapter discusses the prospects for development finance and presents some ideas to improve the inclusiveness of current international aid and financing mechanisms, including new definitions of aid and development finance; the advantages of bilateralism and multilateralism; the requirements for "true development partnership"; developing communities of "common fate and destination"; the intersection of national interest and global public goods; the logic of

---

Box 8.1 (*Cont.*)

using countries' comparative advantages in aid and cooperation; and learning and experimenting in international affairs in
a world full of uncertainty and information asymmetry.

In a multipolar world, diverse ideas and theories for
development are inevitable, as are different types of multilateral development banks and funds complementing and
cooperating with each other. The "new multilateralism,"
epitomized by the One Belt, One Road initiative and the
new development banks and funds, if coordinated and run
well, would be a multiple win for a more peaceful and
prosperous world.

Development Finance in the 21st Century

Who Will Be the New Development Financiers?

In September 2015, the United Nations adopted a resolution to
establish the Sustainable Development Goals (SDGs) for the post-
2015 era. At the Paris climate conference in December 2015
(COP21), 195 countries came together to adopt the first universal
and legally binding global climate deal. The agreement sets out a
global action plan to put the world on track to avoid dangerous
climate change by limiting global warming to well below 2 degrees
Celsius. Now all eyes are on how to finance these endeavors.

In our view, the world economy is facing huge uncertainty and
volatility. Some economists discuss the possibility of secular stagnation; others even speculate on another financial crisis around the
corner. For the developing world, we are cautiously optimistic about
their growth. They have many good opportunities for productivity-
enhancing investment in industrial upgrading, and transaction cost–
reducing investment in releasing infrastructure bottlenecks. Such

investments can not only create jobs and support consumption in the short run, but can also contribute to inclusive and sustainable growth in the long run.

China and other emerging market economies with a sound fiscal position and adequate savings and foreign reserves can go beyond Keynesianism to invest in bottleneck-releasing infrastructure to off-set external shocks and maintain reasonably high growth in the coming years. Other low-income developing countries will also be able to maintain reasonable growth, generate jobs, and contribute to realizing the SDGs – if the global development financial community can mobilize public and private financial resources innovatively in a win-win format. In an interconnected world, achieving higher growth in developing countries is also good for developed countries because they will become larger markets for developed country goods and services, generating jobs and growth in developed countries.

As some established donors are constrained by their heavy debt burden and slow growth in the post-2015 era, development finance will come less from official development assistance (ODA) but more from the other official flows (OOF), OOF-like loans, and OOF-like investments from development banks and sovereign wealth funds in emerging economies. Figure 8.1 compares global savings rates among China, developing countries (excluding China), and developed countries. It is clear that developing countries have much higher savings rate, and thus will have higher investment rates in the next fifteen years (2015–2030). The share of developing countries in global investment (including China) is projected to overtake that of the high-income countries in 2015 and beyond (Figure 8.2), and the shares of emerging market economies in world financial assets and GDP are expected to rise by about 10 percentage points (Table 8.1).

We therefore propose to expand the definitions of development finance, which could induce more contributions from sovereign wealth funds (SWFs) and other public and private entities. Some may ask, why fix something that is not broken?

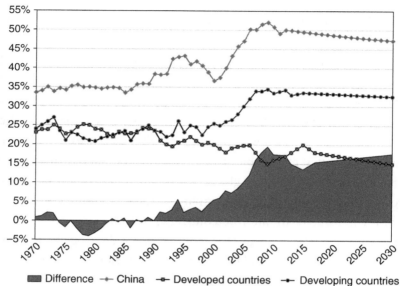

Figure 8.1 Global savings rates for high-income and developing countries,
1970–2030
Source: Updated by the authors based on World Bank Global Development
Horizons (2013).

First, the OECD–DAC definition is far from meeting the needs of
the post-2015 world, when everyone realizes the huge financial gaps
in meeting the SDG and COP21 goals. The credibility and relevance
of ODA for global development have been questioned by OECD
members themselves (Hynes and Scott 2013; OECD-DAC 2014b).
The concept of ODA has been under criticism in recent years, and
the OECD publicly opened the debate in December 2012
(Boussichas and Guillaumont 2014). Many new proposals to reform
the current OECD–DAC concepts have been proposed (Xu and
Carey 2015b; OECD–DAC 2014a, b, and c).

Second, with many emerging market economies continuing to
grow relatively more rapidly and save a large proportion of their
income, the prospect of South-South Development Cooperation is

TABLE 8.1 *Projected emerging market economies' share of world financial assets and GDP*

	Financial Assets			GDP		
	2010	2030	2040 $trn	2010	2030	2030 $trn
Rapid Growth	22%	39%	$223.9	37%	45%	$58.8
Gradual Growth	22%	28%	$156.4	37%	36%	$45.6

Source: Sheng (2013).

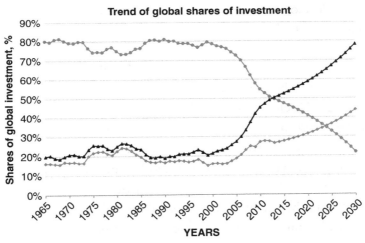

Trend of global shares of investment

— Share of developed countries
— Share of developing countries without China
— Share of developing countries with China

Figure 8.2 Global shares of investment, with developing countries, including China, overtaking the high-income countries, 1965–2030
Source: Authors' projections based on World Bank Global Development Horizons (2013).

likely to expand. China's official stance – as reflected in President Xi Jinping's speech at the UN Assembly in September 2015 and his speech at the sixth FOCAC meeting in Johannesburg – is to renew the confidence in China's approaches to South-South Development

Cooperation, stressing "blood creation" rather than "blood transfusion" (Freeman 2012). He emphasized government-led investment in hard and soft infrastructure and industrial upgrading, as well as deeper doubts about the Western donor approach of providing "aid with conditionality" (Chapter 3).

To "integrate" emerging economies into a global support system for development and to lower the transaction costs requires keeping an open mind on the Chinese and other emerging market economies' perspective about international development, especially allowing for developing countries to help each other on the basis of "equality, mutual respect, reciprocity, and mutual benefit."

Redefining Development Finance

We propose to broaden the definitions of development finance. The OECD–DAC definitions of ODA and OOFs are a good starting point, but they need to be reformed to clarify and to take into account all forms of finance aimed to support development.[1] For monetary policy instruments, there are M0, M1, M2, and M3. In development finance, we can define DF1, DF2, DF3, and DF4 similarly (see just below) according to the extent of "concessionality" with a consistent benchmark market interest rate; the source (the extent of "official" or state involvement); the destination countries (low- or middle-income developing countries); and the objectives of the financing (for economic development and welfare). Similar ideas were also seen in previous studies (Braütigam 2011a; Center for Global Development's China-aid database;[2] OECD–DAC 2014; Boussichas and Guillaumont 2014; and Xu and Carey 2015b). A new set of clearer definitions would facilitate transparency, accountability, and selectivity by development partners, encourage SWFs to invest in developing countries, and facilitate public-private partnerships in developing-country infrastructure.

In particular, SWFs are managing huge amount of assets, in excess of US$21 trillion, and many of them are seeking higher risk-adjusted returns.[3] Some of them have traditionally underinvested in the emerging and developing countries, with less than 10 percent of assets allocated to these countries. Norway, for example, is having a national debate on how best to reallocate some of its huge assets to developing countries. The Norwegian Government Pension Fund is the world's second largest SWF after the United States, with US $888 billion in assets and is expected to grow to more than US$1,100 billion by 2020. But it allocates 90 percent of assets to "liquid" developed-country equities, with a real rate of return of mere 3.17 percent since 1998, much lower than other SWFs with more significant investment in emerging markets, which are in the range of 10 percent or more (Kapoor 2013; Box 8.2). NorFund in contrast, a much smaller Norwegian fund investing in developing countries, has a higher rate of return than the Norwegian Government Pension Fund (GPF). Redefining "development finance," as we propose, would help sway public opinion toward SWFs investing in developing countries and expand the sources of development finance. See also Temasek's experience in Box 8.2.

We propose to redefine development finance in the following ways (Figure 8.3):

- DF1 = Official Development Assistance (ODA, as defined by OECD–DAC with reforms as proposed in the December 16, 2014 decision and more recently).
- DF2 = DF1+OOF including preferential export buyer's credits.
- DF3 = DF2+OOF-like loans (non-concessional loans from state entities for development but at market interest rates).
- DF4 = DF3+OOF-like investment (equity investments by SWFs, development projects supported by state guarantees, and PPP projects for public infrastructure, which provide global/national public goods for sustainable development). This latter concept would be broadly consistent with but uniquely different from Total Official Support for Sustainable Development (TOSSD) proposed by OECD–DAC.[4]

Box 8.2 Temasek's experience in obtaining high returns by investing in emerging market and developing countries

Temasek Holdings Private Limited (Temasek) is an investment company owned by the Government of Singapore. Established in 1974, it now owns and manages a net portfolio of US$180 billion (as of March 31, 2016), mainly in Singapore and Asia. Required to follow the international guideline for sovereign wealth funds, it is one of a few global firms assigned with the highest overall corporate credit ratings of AAA by Standard & Poor's and Aaa by Moody's.

With significant portfolio investment in emerging and developing Asia, Temasek's financial performance is stellar: Its annual shareholder return has been 15 percent since inception, much higher than other SWFs investing purely in industrial countries. By geographic allocation, Asia (excluding Singapore) accounted for about 40 percent of Temasek's portfolio (in which China accounted for 25 percent), followed by North America and Europe with a combined 31 percent share of their new investments. Temasek's experience should be valuable to all countries with a SWF or national development company.

If all SWFs invest more in developing countries and increase their allocation to low-income developing countries by 5 or more percentage points of their assets, that would be sufficient to release bottlenecks in those countries.

Source: Authors based on Temasek Review 2016. http://www.temasekreview.com.sg/

We draw special attention to the unconventional development assistance provided by southern partners, such as "turnkey projects," "real sector (barter) exchanges," and "resource-financed infrastructure"

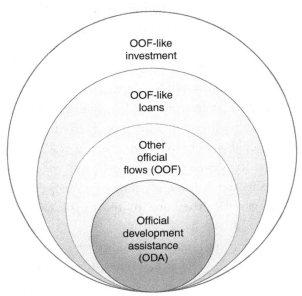

Figure 8.3 Expanding the definition of development finance
Notes: The circles correspond to DF1 = ODA; DF2=ODA+OOF; DF3=DF2
+ OOF-like loans; and DF4=DF3+OOF-like investment. Another category
could be added separately for SSDC that cannot be monetized.
Source: Authors.

(RFI). The RFI concept can help connect a developing country's comparative advantage, such as resource extraction, with the construction of bottleneck-releasing infrastructure – two otherwise separate supply chains – thus reducing transaction costs and making public infrastructure more attractive to the private sector.

For example, China agreed to use Ghana's cocoa exports (a comparative advantage) as collateral for its loans for building a hydropower station (Box 8.4). "An RFI credit may be the least-cost option for obtaining essential infrastructure that cannot generate sufficient revenue to support a project finance transaction" (Lin and Wang, quoted in in World Bank 2014, p. 76).[5] Some elements of SSDC cannot be monetized, such as the number of medical doctors, teachers, agricultural experts, and engineers, but separate categories can be established for them.

Volumes and Global Governance

The volume of international development finance depends heavily on institutional arrangements, the channels of financing and coordination, and ultimately the global environment and the structure of global governance. In other words, it depends on whether SSDC or development finance are welcome, whether and how much the voices of emerging market partners are included, and whether they are invited to the table for shaping the global "rules of the road."

China's development finance depends on many factors. A rough projection method is to use China's forecast growth rate in the next 10 years and use the proportion of development finance to gross national income. According to one study by staff of the People's Bank of China, estimated outward investment in infrastructure "will not be less than US$100 billion annually (RMB 630 billion yuan)" (Jin 2012, p. 62). "Considering the increased potential, China could well afford to have outward investment of RMB 600 billion to RMB 1000 billion yuan per year. Assume that this amount consists of 95 percent in loans and equity investment, and 5 percent in grant, this means that China's Ministry of Finance will need to budget RMB 30 billion to 50 billion yuan for international aid. This number is only about 0.3 percent to 0.5 percent of China's 2011 fiscal revenue, accounting for less than 0.1 percent of GDP, much lower than the fiscal burden of the Marshall Plan (to the US Treasury)" (Jin 2012, p. 62).[6]

In our view, as China's GNI and fiscal revenue continue to grow, the amount of development finance (in our broad definition) will rise dramatically, to close to US$100 billion in 2015–2016 (including grants, concessional loans, and export buyer credits, other concessional loans, nonconcessional loans for infrastructure, as well as contributions to the Silk Road Fund, AIIB, New Development Bank, and other multilateral banks). As shown by its recent commitments, China will gradually take more responsibilities and explore its new roles in global affairs. Its share of development finance in GNI is thus likely to grow steeply to 0.3 percent of GNI or more. However, the pace of increase depends on the global governance system. China has tried to set up the "right" platforms for its contribution to global development, including its contribution to setting up the AIIB and other new groupings such as the New Development Bank and the Silk Road Fund (Boxes 8.5 and 8.6), as well as launching its One Belt, One Road vision. We expect that similar multilateral or plurilateral banks and funds may emerge in the future.

The One Belt, One Road Vision, and Confucianism

Chinese President Xi Jinping at the APEC summit in 2013 proposed a new vision to build a "one silk road economic belt and a maritime silk road" (One Belt, One Road for short), supported by more than 50 countries along the proposed routes (Figure 8.4). What is its rationale?

The One Belt, One Road idea reflects Chinese leaders' vision of a world order guided by shared prosperity, "peaceful co-existence with differences," and commitments for providing global public goods, peace and security, and sustainability, drawing on China's deep wealth of Confucianism. Most historians agree that China was relatively prosperous before the industrial revolution. "Until the Industrial Revolution, China was far richer. In fact, China produced a greater share of total world GDP than any western society in 18 of the last 20 centuries. As late as 1820, it produced over 30 percent of world GDP – an amount exceeding the GDP of Western Europe, Eastern Europe, and the United States combined" (Kissinger 2011, p. 11).

Confucianism may explain why. "As early as the Song Dynasty (960–1279), China led the world in nautical technology; its fleets

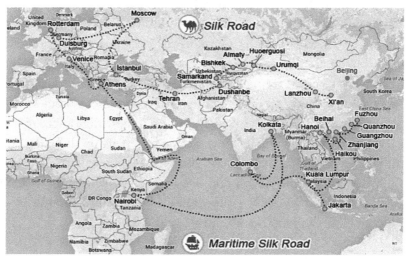

Figure 8.4 The One Belt, One Road route variants
Source: Xinhua.

could have carried the empire into an era of conquest and exploration. Yet China acquired no overseas colonies and showed relatively little interest in the countries beyond its coast" (Kissinger 2011, p. 8).

Confucius emphasized *ren* (benevolence); the cultivation of social harmony; the principles of compassionate rule, including his love of lifelong learning, as in "It is indeed a pleasure to acquire knowledge and as you go on acquiring, to put into practice what you have acquired,"[7] and through learning from others: "When I walk along with two others, they may serve me as my teachers. I will select their good qualities and follow them, their bad qualities and avoid them."[8]

As Kissinger noted, "China owed its millennial survival far less to the punishments meted out by its Emperors than to the community of values fostered among its population and its government of scholar-officials" (2011, p.13). The civil service examination allowed talented people to become members of the ruling class, which brought handsome economic returns and high honor to their families. Moreover, the examinations instilled a set of values, emphasizing the loyalty to the emperors and the services to the people, in the mind of elites further reduced the costs of ruling and holding the large country together (Lin 1995). This community of values helped hold a large country together for thousands of years.[9]

Confucianism also shaped China's relations with its neighbors. Instead of using its power to conquer them, China used its power to restore and maintain peace with them, reflecting the principles of Confucianism to "revive states that had been extinguished and restore families whose line of succession had been broken, and called to office those who had retired into obscurity, so as to gain the hearts of the people in the world" (《论语·尧曰》：“兴灭国，继绝世，举逸民，天下之民归心焉). This might help to explain why "China acquired no overseas colonies and showed relatively little interest in the countries beyond its coast" (Kissinger 2011, p. 8).

Deeply rooted in China's history and civilization is a firm belief that "one should not impose on others what oneself does not desire"[10] and "one wishing to be successful oneself must also help others to be successful; one who wishes to develop oneself also hopes to help others develop." These principles have been behind the visions guiding China's foreign aid and cooperation in the last 50 years.

The new generation of Chinese leaders has attempted to modernize and strengthen these values and principles. "China now has its basic interest and responsibility in the systemic functioning of global development financing" (Xu and Carey 2015a). And as Chinese President Xi has said, "The vast Pacific Ocean has ample space for China and the United States" (Xi, 2012). These ideas have been fully incorporated in China's thirteenth Five Year Plan, which calls for a new pattern of development based on five principles: "innovation, coordination, green, open and shared development." It sets a strategy of two-way openness, promoting orderly movement of all production elements, supporting infrastructure development and connectivity with neighboring countries (National People's Congress 2015).

In other words, this One Belt, One Road will not be just a vision, but a guiding principle in China's foreign policy and development finance, with a concrete action plan.

A New Bilateral Approach: Building Communities of "Common Fate and Destination"

BRICS countries and other non-DAC member countries will continue their bilateral approach in South-South Development Cooperation (SSDC), as the Addis Ababa Action Agenda has supported it, for reducing poverty and reaching the Sustainable Development Goals (Box 8.3). But to overcome some of the incentive problems and the information-asymmetry and principal-agent problems that exist in the "aid effectiveness" literature (Chapter 1), the following principles should be followed:

Host countries must have full ownership of their development programs. An SSDC project should be "requested by the host country, led by the host country, and co-constructed by the host country." Both providers and hosts are on equal footing, and either one of them can say no (Addis Ababa Action Agenda, article 56).

The partners of cooperation may seek to establish communities of "common fate and destination" to find common ground of interest that can benefit both partner- and host- country national interest (Figure 8.5). Admittedly, each developing country has its national interest, and SSDC is not purely altruistic. Both sides should strive to seek common ground of interest and reach mutual benefit and a win-win outcome. At project level, a joint venture company may be or should be established before capital can be injected and loans can be borrowed. In fact, this joint venture is the embodiment of this community of "common destination." For example, in the case of a high-speed rail system

---

Box 8.3 The Addis Ababa Action Agenda of the Third International Conference on Financing for Development supports South-South Cooperation

"55. We will hold open, inclusive and transparent discussions on the modernization of the ODA measurement and on the proposed measure of "total official support for sustainable development" (TOSSD) and we affirm that any such measure will not dilute commitments already made."

"56. South-South cooperation is an important element of international cooperation for development as a complement, not a substitute, to North-South cooperation. We recognize its increased importance, different history and particularities and stress that South-South cooperation should be seen as an expression of solidarity among peoples and countries of the South, based on their shared experiences and objectives. It should continue to be guided by the principles of respect for national sovereignty, national ownership and independence, equality, nonconditionality, noninterference in domestic affairs and mutual benefit."

"57. We welcome the increased contributions of South-South cooperation to poverty eradication and sustainable development. We encourage developing countries to voluntarily step up their efforts to strengthen South-South cooperation and to further improve its development effectiveness ... "

---

in Indonesia, a Chinese company selected by international competitive bidding will form a joint venture with the Indonesian Railway Company – each agreeing to contribute to the equity capital. Then other lenders and investors, like China Development Bank and the Silk Road Fund, may contribute to the equity capital as well. In this way, both sides can benefit if the project succeeds, and both sides will lose if the project fails.

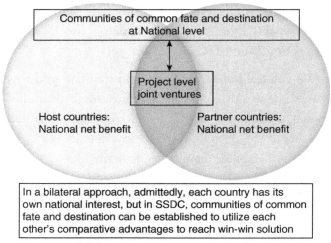

Figure 8.5 Communities of common fate and destination – and
project-level joint ventures
Source: Authors.

In bilateral SSDC, trade and aid and investment can be better combined if both sides agree. For example, if a developing country decides to build a hydropower dam, which requires a huge amount of financing, the government can select a qualified company through international competitive bidding. Usually the country with demonstrated comparative advantage will win the bid, and it can mobilize financing through combining export buyer credits and non-concessional loans. Naturally, this syndicated loan (concessional or non-concessional) may be tied to the services provided by the company that won the bid. For the Bui Dam in Ghana, using export proceeds from cocoa beans as collateral for the loan is leveraging Ghana's comparative advantage in a smart way to get the urgently needed power. Both sides benefited (Box 8.4). Combining trade with aid and cooperation, the comparative advantage will be better used, and both sides will benefit from this commercial deal. Similarly, other countries facing similar foreign exchange constraints can use

Box 8.4 Leveraging Ghana's comparative advantage for Bui Dam

Bui Dam is a gravity roller-compacted concrete dam constructed at the Bui National Park, in Ghana. With its completion in 2013, the dam is generating 400MW of power and facilitating irrigation of about 30,000 ha of land.

The total project cost was initially estimated to be US$622 million, upped by US$168 million later. It is being financed by the government of Ghana's own resources (US$60 million) and two credits by China Exim Bank: a concessional loan of US$270 million at 2 percent interest and a commercial loan of US$292 million. Both loans have a grace period of five years and an amortization period of 20 years. The proceeds of 30,000 tons a year of Ghanaian cocoa exports to China, which are placed in an escrow account at the Exim Bank, serve as collateral for the loan. Once the dam became operational, 85 percent of the proceeds of electricity sales from the hydropower plant goes to the escrow account. If not all the proceeds are needed to service the loan, the remainder reverts to the government of Ghana.

The dam was completed by the Sino Hydro Corporation as part of an Engineering, Procurement and Construction (EPC) Turnkey Project Contract. Bui Power Authority owns and manages the dam. Sino Hydro won the bid of the project with funding from the Chinese Exim Bank in 2005, followed by an environmental impact assessment and a feasibility study.

The Bui hydropower plant increases the installed electricity generation capacity in Ghana by 22 percent, from 1,920 MW in 2008 to 2,360 MW. It alleviates the severe power shortages common in Ghana. In addition to generating power, the Bui Dam will provide water for irrigation and also improve tourism and fishing in Ghana. The full development impact has yet to be carefully measured and analyzed.

Source: Lin and Wang 2013.

this "resource-financed infrastructure" approach to achieve their own development objectives.

But bilateral SSDC has disadvantages. Obviously, it cannot leverage funds and share risks among multiple partner countries. Nor does it facilitate learning and trilateral cooperation, so improving its effectiveness through learning remains a question mark. And in the event of a dispute or default, it is difficult to resolve.

Most important, bilateral mechanisms are completely inadequate for providing global public goods. Similarly, plurilateral arrangements (among a few partners, as with the BRICS) are insufficient to solve such global issues such as climate change, and interregional connectivity – hence, the need to resort to a multilateral system.

Plurilateral Financial Arrangements

Brazil, Russia, India, China, and South Africa (BRICS) have jointly established the New Development Bank, formerly the BRICS Bank, headed by an experienced Indian Banker, K.V. Kamath, with headquarters in Shanghai. In its first articles of agreement, it states the objective of "mobilizing resources for infrastructure and sustainable development project in BRICS and other emerging economies and developing countries, complementing the existing efforts of multilateral and regional financial institutions for global growth and development."

The BRICS are in different continents, with different comparative advantages and different national interests. Many analysts concluded that the New Development Bank is "temporary and weak." We think they are wrong. We believe this bank reflects a true partnership of equals, based on the principle of "peaceful co-existence with differences." It also has the potential to become a "community of common fate and destination." These five countries are all middle-income countries striving to upgrade their industries from their own positions in the world's value chains. They have own national interests but also large grounds for common interest. They are teammates in climbing the same mountain of structural transformation and need help from each other. And with their different comparative advantages, they can complement each other economically.

Similarly, on governance, all founding member countries contribute equally to the New Development Bank and have equal voting rights – a "true partnership in development." "The voting power of each member shall be equal to the number of its subscribed shares in the capital stock of the Bank" (New Development Bank 2014). No one is in dominating position, to impose conditions on other partners, but all will follow the international rules of the game. Partners have the freedom to join or exit, and each can say yes or no. Membership is also open to all members of the United Nations.

Brazil, China, and India see themselves as development partners, not donors. Their experiences as recipients of traditional development assistance and their identification with other recipients contribute to their sensitivity to the term "aid." Conditionality, they argue, would undermine the principles of respecting national sovereignty and promoting solidarity. In fact, these countries have differences in their SSDC, as highlighted by Mwase and Yang (2012, section 4.1). BRIC financing has helped alleviate infrastructure bottlenecks in many low-income countries and should help them tap their natural resources. Such financing has benefits – it has resulted in a 35 percent improvement in electricity supply, a 10 percent increase in rail capacity, and lower prices of telephone services (Foster et al. 2009; Onjala 2008). At least 35 countries in sub-Saharan Africa have benefited from or are discussing Chinese infrastructure financing (Doemeland et al. 2010).

In sum, there is ample room for mutual learning and exchanges of experience among the BRICS, the traditional and emerging suppliers of development cooperation, and the bilateral and the new and old multilateral financial organizations.

Advantages of the New Multilateralism

China's transition from a largely bilateral approach to being involved in a new multilateralism – South-led multilateralism – is a win-win for itself and the world. In the past, most development cooperation from China was bilateral (Chapter 3).

With the newly established multilateral financial organizations, China will contribute more development finance. International development is a new area for China – one cannot learn how to swim without jumping into the water – and it offers six main advantages.

Initiating and running a new multilateral financial institution will be a learning and experiment process for China. A new group of Chinese will take leadership roles in the New Development Bank (NDB) and the Asian Infrastructure Investment Bank (AIIB), led by its president Mr. Jin Liqun, and working with their colleagues will enhance their international leadership and coordination skills.

A multilateral financial institution allows China to leverage capital and pool a larger amount of capital, exerting a larger impact than through bilateral development cooperation. This will reduce the amount of capital flowing from developing countries to developed countries and improve the efficiency of global capital allocation. Theoretically this will improve the rate of return, since investing in the bottlenecks of developing countries should have higher rates of return than investing in industrial countries, where capital is abundant. It also allows better risk-sharing among a larger number of member countries, which is good for risk management. Moreover, it enhances shareholders' ability to protect their investment against all sorts of risks, including political risk.

The rest of the world can benefit from the large savings, rapidly growing consumer demand, and scale economies of the very large

BRICS economies. China, India, and other emerging countries are at a stage where labor-intensive industries need to relocate to other countries due to sharply rising labor costs at home (Chapter 2). This provides huge opportunities for low-income countries to upgrade their manufacturing industries.

In addition, China enjoys scale economies that other smaller countries do not, which lets it keep down construction costs of large transport networks (see Box 5.3 on high-speed rail). China has demonstrated its comparative advantage in constructing large infrastructure, thanks to its inexpensive labor and engineers, the capacity to complete many large projects domestically, and the ability to raise funds and implement large projects in other parts of the world (Chapter 5). Countries connecting with China and Chinese rail networks can benefit from these scale economies and comparative advantages, increasing their access to inland consumer markets. Indeed, the social benefits of connecting to a large (hard and soft) network should be huge.

The new institutions require all shareholders to share information and thus enhance transparency and internal governance. This will later influence the behavior of large shareholders domestically and provide pressure mechanisms for law making in domestic reforms. For example, in setting up the governance structure of the AIIB, Chinese leaders will learn from other founding member countries that have a more complete system of foreign aid laws and regulation. The Articles of Agreement of the NDB and the AIIB presage the highest standards of transparency and governance, which should influence those in bilateral SSDC. This will enhance trust among all founding members, including that between southern and northern partners.

The articles of agreement of the AIIB stress the freedom to use all currencies in the Bank's operations. Article 19 stipulates that "Members shall not impose any restrictions on currencies, including the receipt, holding or transfer by the Bank or by any recipient from the Bank, for payments in a country."[11] Both the NDB and the AIIB could potentially issue renminbi bonds (or other local currency bonds) and grant renminbi loans if their shareholders want to. This will, to some extent, release the foreign exchange constraints and currency mismatches that developing countries face. In the long term, Article 19 may engender more widespread use of currencies from emerging market countries. In November 2015, the IMF agreed to include the renminbi as one of the five components of Special Drawing Right (SDR), and central banks are likely to hold renminbi in their international reserves. In the long term, the international use of renminbi as an investment instrument will increase.

China's approach to development cooperation has advantages. China combines trade, aid, and investment to assist other developing countries in gaining capacity for self-development, building the necessary hard and soft infrastructure needed for structural transformation. Southern countries such as BRICS are closer culturally and economically to many low-income developing countries, with greater complementarity. Their development cooperation approach in a multilateral development bank or fund can improve the aid effectiveness over the northern countries' approach of aid with conditionality, and thus benefit development. Development partners, whether from North or South, working together in multilateral organizations, can thus offer win-win-win solutions.

G-20 and Global Governance

The G-20, representing economies accounting for about 85 percent of global output, has grown to be the world's premier forum for economic policy cooperation. The G-20 summit, set up at the height of the global financial crisis in 2008, demonstrated global leaders' determination to work together and put the global economy back on its feet.

The G-20 summit has become an indispensible platform for voicing developing country concerns and reforming the global financial

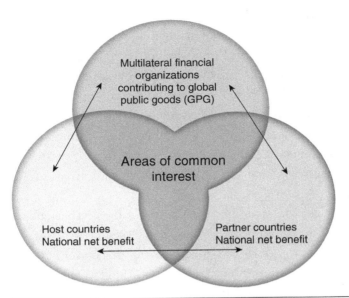

Comparing to bilateral or plurilateral approaches, the new multilateralism can expand the intersection areas of common interests, improve information flow, learning and transparency among all partners in order to reach win-win-win solutions on global issues.

Figure 8.6 The new multilateralism can expand areas of common interest
Source: Authors.

architecture and global governance. For example, in Pittsburgh, Pennsylvania, in 2009, in the midst of the global financial crisis, the G-20 proposed to increase the voice and representation of developing countries, and to enhance economic cooperation between the global South and North. In Seoul, Republic of Korea, in 2010, development cooperation was at the top of its agenda. In Brisbane, Australia, in 2014, infrastructure development was considered key to global recovery. And in Antalya, Turkey, in 2015, leaders committed to undertake concrete actions to strengthen the global economy, make global growth more inclusive, enhance the resilience of the international financial system, mobilize investment to raise long-term growth, and implement previous commitments on economic reform and labor markets.

In 2016, the G-20 summit was hosted by China in Hangzhou in September. It has offered a good opportunity for Chinese scholars, think tanks, and policymakers to formulate and voice new ideas for global growth and sustainable development, including our ideas based on the New Structural Economics. This year's G-20 theme was "Towards an Innovative, Invigorated, Interconnected, and Inclusive World Economy." Among the long list of outcome documents, we see the work of the G-20 Development Working Group as most relevant to the topic of this book.

Development has long been at the top of the G-20 agenda. The G-20 has strongly supported the 2030 Agenda for Sustainable Development and achieved much in infrastructure investment, food security, taxation, financial inclusion, human resource development, and so on. This year, in addition to the long list of priorities including employment generation and poverty eradication, special attention has been attached to supporting industrialization in Africa and other developing countries.

We are delighted that G-20 outcome document (G20 Leaders' Communique Hangzhou Summit) points out that Industrialization is vital to each country's development. In particular, at least 3 components are most relevant to the topic of this book: those on industrialization, on infrastructure, and on global governance. In addition to article 13 on New Industrialization, article 35 on Africa's industrialization is most critical to our work on SSDC.

"35. We launch the G20 Initiative on Supporting Industrialization in Africa and LDCs to strengthen their inclusive growth and development potential through voluntary policy options including: promoting inclusive and sustainable structural transformation; supporting sustainable agriculture, agri-business and agro-industry development; deepening, broadening and updating the local knowledge and production base; promoting investment in sustainable and secure energy, including renewables and energy efficiency; exploring ways to develop cooperation on industrial production and vocational training and sustainable and resilient infrastructure and industries; supporting industrialization through trade in accordance with WTO rules; and leveraging domestic and external finance and supporting equitable access to finance – with a focus on women and youth; and promoting science, technology and innovation as critical means for industrialization."

Second, the section on Inclusive and interconnectivity reflected the influence of China's experience, as explained earlier.

"39. We reaffirm our commitment to promote investment with focus on infrastructure in terms of both quantity and quality. We welcome the Joint Declaration of Aspirations on Actions to Support Infrastructure Investment by 11 multilateral development banks (MDBs), including their announcements of quantitative ambitions for high-quality infrastructure projects within their respective institutional mandates as well as their efforts to maximize the quality of infrastructure projects, strengthen project pipelines, collaborate further among existing and new MDBs, strengthen the enabling environment for infrastructure investment in developing countries, as well as catalyze private resources."

On global governance, the following statements are particularly timely and critical – they reflect those voices from China and emerging market economies. They also confirm China's efforts to promote new multilateralism by joining the existing systems.

- "We welcome the entry into effect of the 2010 IMF quota and governance reform and are working towards the completion of the 15th General Review of Quotas, including a new quota formula, by the 2017 Annual Meetings.
- We reaffirm that any realignment under the 15th review in quota shares is expected to result in increased shares for dynamic economies in line with their relative positions in the world economy, and hence likely in the share of emerging market and developing countries as a whole. We are committed to protecting the voice and representation of the poorest members.

- We support the World Bank Group to implement its shareholding review according to the agreed roadmap, timeframe and principles, with the objective of achieving equitable voting power over time.
- We underline the importance of promoting sound and sustainable financing practices and will continue to improve debt restructuring processes. We support the continued effort to incorporate the enhanced contractual clauses into sovereign bonds.
- We support the Paris Club's discussion of a range of sovereign debt issues, and the ongoing work of the Paris Club, as the principal international forum for restructuring official bilateral debt, towards the broader inclusion of emerging creditors. We welcome the admission of the Republic of Korea and the decision of Brazil to join the Paris Club. **We welcome China's continued regular participation in Paris Club meetings and intention to play a more constructive role**, including further discussions on potential membership.
- Following the IMF's decision, we welcome the inclusion of the RMB into the Special Drawing Right (SDR) currency basket on October 1st. We support the ongoing examination of the broader use of the SDR, such as broader reporting in the SDR and the issuance of SDR-denominated bonds, as a way to enhance resilience. In this context, we take note of the recent issuance of SDR bonds by the World Bank in China's interbank market. We welcome further work by the international organizations to support the development of local currency bond markets, including intensifying efforts to support low-income countries." (G20 Leaders' Communique Hangzhou Summit, 4-5 September 2016).

The ideas in this book are relevant to implementing these G-20 Outcome items, and G-20 agenda in the future. They underscore the importance of structural transformation, linking the New Structural Economics with China's approach to South-South Development Cooperation – using its comparative advantages in helping releasing infrastructure bottlenecks and investing in light manufacturing industries in Africa and other developing countries. In addition, our work to help African countries identify their latent comparative advantage through the Growth Identification and Facilitation framework provides a foundation for discussions at the G-20 summits. To coordinate SSDC with the ODA definition of established donors, our proposed expansion of the ODA definition to DF1, DF2, DF3, and DF4 could improve transparency, facilitate coordination and accountability, and sway public opinion to invest in the global public goods and increase interconnectivity. And our proposal to establish a monitoring and evaluation system to rank all partners, banks, and companies could also be discussed in future G-20 summits.

Conclusions

We believe that most low-income countries will witness a significant structural transformation in the post-2015 era if all emerging and established development partners work together for the benefit of these countries.

To be effective, aid or development cooperation must be in the host country's own interest and demand driven. Combining aid, trade, and investment – a market-based approach – can ensure the alignment of incentives among equal partners, as shown by the successful experiences in many East Asian countries.

China needs to continue to learn to become a better development partner by listening to the voices from partners and interacting with the governments, NGOs, and civil societies. It also needs to be more open and transparent in providing accurate data on international development finance and activities. Our view is that any deals made in the dark are more likely to be revoked or renegotiated by a client country's next government. The political economy dynamics must thus be taken into consideration when discussing with the current government of the client country.

Through plurilateral and multilateral financial organizations, China and other stakeholders will learn from each other and build communities of common fate and destination. They can use their different comparative advantages and complement each other to facilitate their structural transformations. The multilateral arrangement can also provide pressure for legal and institutional reforms domestically to improve transparency, governance, and social and environmental standards in each of the partner countries.

The established OECD donors also need to see whether China's approach provides useful lessons to improve the effectiveness of the conventional North-South aid. A recent study by the World Bank (2014) reviewing Resource for Infrastructure (RFI) deals finds that they can be more effective in advancing the developmental impact many years ahead of the conventional North-South approaches. Many African leaders find China's approach (in RFI) more desirable since it can lead to inexpensive and tangible results within a time span of three or four years, coinciding with the political cycle in a democracy.

In the post-2015 era, development finance will come less from ODA but more from the other official flows (OOF), OOF-like loans, and OOF-like investments from development banks, sovereign wealth funds, and emerging economies. That is why we propose expanding the definitions of development finance, which could induce more contributions from SWFs and other public or private entities. The recent OECD–DAC decision to introduce a new and broader concept of Total Official Support for Sustainable Development (TOSSD) is in the right direction, though the details have yet to be worked out, discussed, and agreed upon.

We are optimistic that a common ground can be found for partners from the North and the South to work together as shown by the G-20 outcome documents on multiple win solutions for structural transformation to achieve sustainable development in the South. If all countries work together investing in bottleneck-releasing infrastructure and providing global public goods, including China's One Belt, One Road initiative and 10 proposals for Africa, the prospects for achieving global peace and development will be enhanced.

Notes

1. Debate is sharp on calculating concessional loans, whether face value (OECD-DAC approach) or budget subsidies (China approach) should be used, or what interest rate should be used as the discount rate. Li Ruogu claims that "all China's loans for development [from Eximbank of China] are concessional in character" if a "proper" benchmark interest rate can be used for the discount rate (Li 2007).

2. This useful 2013 database is available at http://china.aiddata.org/.

3. SWF Institute, accessed October 2015. Available at http://www.swfinstitute.org/fund-rankings/.

4. At the time of writing this book (2015), OECD was still discussing the concept of TOSSD. A new publication has just come out for the concept of TOSSD, and how to measure it. See OECD's June 2016, "TOSSD Compendium," available at http://www.oecd.org/dac/financing-sustainable-development/TOSSD Compendium2016.pdf.

5. The RFI model allows the exchange of one resource for another productive asset in the long term and thus support real sector diversification without relying completely on the financial market. In addition, it reduces the leakages due to resource revenues being transferred out of the developing country, or capital flight. This "real-for-real" exchange could help overcome severe financial and governance constraints suffered by low-income but resource-rich countries (Lin and Wang in World Bank 2014, p. 76).

6. Note that this projection included grants, grant elements of concessional loans, and the total amount that can be leveraged by the Ministry of Finance, for investing in developing countries' infrastructure, implying a broad definition of development financing.

7. Lunyu-Xueer.《论语·学而》

8. Lunyu-Shuer.《论语·述而》

9. On Chinese value system see Sun 1929, and Lin 1995, among others.

10. "己所不欲，勿施於人。" can be translated as *"What you do not wish for yourself, do not do to others."* Zi Gong (a disciple of Confucius) asked: *"Is there any one word that could guide a person throughout life?" The Master replied: "How about 'shu' [reciprocity]: never impose on others what you would not choose for yourself?"* –Confucius, *Analects* XV.24.

11. AIIB, Articles of Agreement, article 19. Available at http://www.aiib.org/uploadfile/2015/0814/20150814022158430.pdf.

Bibliography

Acemoglu, D., S. Johnson, and J. Robinson. 2005. "Institutions as a Fundamental Cause of Long-Run Growth." *Handbook of Economic Growth vol. 1A*. North Holland: Elsevier.

Acemoglu, D., and J. Robinson. 2012. *Why Nations Fail: The Origins of Power, Prosperity and Poverty*. New York: Crown Business.

Aghion, P., M. Dewatripont, L. Du, A. E. Harrison, and P. Legros. 2011. "Industrial Policy and Competition," 18 June. Available at SSRN: http://ssrn.com/abstract=1811643 or http://dx.doi.org/10.2139/ssrn.1811643

AIIB. 2015. "Articles of Agreement." Available at http://www.aiib.org/uploadfile/2015/0814/20150814022158430.pdf

Aiyar, S., and U. Ruthbah. 2008. "Where Did All the Aid Go? An Empirical Analysis of Absorption and Spending." Working Paper WP/08/34, IMF, Washington, DC.

Akamatsu, K. 1935. "Wagakuni yomo kogyohin no susei (Trend of Japan's Wooden Product Industry)." *Shogyo Keizai Ronse (Journal of Nagoya Higher Commercial School)* 13: 129–212.

———. 1961. "A Theory of Unbalanced Growth in the World Economy." *Weltwirtschaftliches Archiv* 86 (2): 196–215.

———. 1962. "A Historical Pattern of Economic Growth in Developing Countries." *The Developing Economies* 1 (s1): 3–25.

Akramov, K. T. 2012. *Foreign Aid Allocation, Governance, and Economic Growth*. Washington, DC: International Food Policy Research Institute.

Akyeampong, E., and L. Xu. 2015. "The Three Phases /Faces of China in Independent Africa: Reconceptualizing China-Africa Engagement." In J. Y. Lin and C. Monga, eds., *The Oxford Handbook of Africa and Economics*. Oxford: Oxford University Press.

Alfaro, L., and A. Charlton. 2014. "Growth and the Quality of Foreign Direct Investment." In J. E. Stiglitz and J. Y. Lin, eds., *The Industrial Policy Revolution I*. London: Palgrave Macmillan.

Aoki, M., K. Murdock, and M. Okuno-Fujiwara. 1997. "Beyond the East Asian Miracle: Introducing the Market-Enhancing View." In M. Aoki, H.-K. Kim, and M. Okuno-Fujiwara, eds., *The Role of Government in East Asian Economic Development*. Oxford: Clarendon Press.

Arndt, C., S. Jones, and F. Tarp. 2010. "Aid, Growth and Development: Have We Come Full Circle?" UNU-WIDER Working Paper 2010/96, United Nations University, World Institute for Development Economics Research, Helsinki.

Arrow, K. J. 1962. "The Economic Implications of Learning by Doing." *Review of Economic Studies* 29 (3): 155–173.

Asian Development Bank and ADBI. 2009. *Infrastructure for a Seamless Asia*. Manila: Asian Development Bank.

Bai, C.-E., C.-T. Hsieh, and Y. Qian 2006. "The Return to Capital in China." Working Paper 12755, National Bureau of Economic Research, Cambridge, MA.

Baissac, C. 2011. "Planned Obsolescence? Export Processing Zones and Structural Reform in Mauritius." In T. Farole and G. Akinci, eds., *Special Economic Zones: Progress, Emerging Challenges, and Future Directions*. Washington, DC: World Bank.

Baker & McKenzie. 2015. *Spanning Africa's Infrastructure Gap: How Development Capital Is Transforming Africa's Project Build-Out*. The Economist Corporate Network, November. Available at: http://ftp01.economist.com.hk/ECN_papers/Infrastructure-Africa

Balassa, B. 1965. "Trade Liberalisation and 'Revealed' Comparative Advantage." *The Manchester School* 33 (2): 99–123.

Barro, R. J. 1998. *Determinants of Economic Growth: A Cross Country Empirical Study*. Cambridge, MA: MIT Press.

Bell, D. A. 2015. *The China Model: Political Meritocracy and the Limits of Democracy*. Princeton: Princeton University Press.

Berg, A., S. Aiyar, M. Hussain, S. Roache, T. Mirzoev, and A. Mahone. 2007. "The Macroeconomics of Scaling Up Aid: Lessons from Recent Experience." IMF Occasional Paper 253, IMF, Washington, DC.

Berg, A., J. Gottschalk, R. Portillo, and L.-F. Zanna. 2010. "The Macroeconomics of Medium-Term Aid Scaling-Up Scenarios." IMF Working Paper 10/160, IMF, Washington, DC.

Blanchard, O., G. Dell'Ariccia and P. Mauro. 2010. "Rethinking Macroeconomic Policy." *Journal of Money, Credit, and Banking* 42 (Suppl.): 199–215.

Blanchard, O., and F. Giavazzi. 2004. "Improving the SGP through a Proper Accounting of Public Investment." CEPR Discussion Paper 4220, Centre for Economic Policy Research, London.

Boone, P. (1996). "Politics and the Effectiveness of Foreign Aid." *European Economic Review* 40(2): 289–329.

Bottelier, P. 2001. "Was World Bank Support for the Qinghai Anti-Poverty Project in China Ill Considered?" *Harvard Asia Quarterly* V (1).

2006. "China and the World Bank: How a Partnership Was Built." Working Paper 277, Stanford Center for International Development.

Boussichas, M., and P. Guillaumont. 2014. "Measuring Official Development Assistance: Why and How to Change." Policy Brief B100, FERDI, Clermont-Ferrand, France.

Boyenge, J. P. S. 2007. "ILO Database on Export Processing Zones, Revised." Working Paper, ILO, Geneva. Available at: http://www.ilo.org/public/libdoc/ilo/2007/107B09_80_engl.pdf.

Braütigam, D. 2009. *The Dragon's Gift: The Real Story of China in Africa.* New York: Oxford University Press.

2011a. "Aid with Chinese Characteristics: Chinese Foreign Aid and Development Finance meet the OECD–DAC Aid Regime." *Journal of International Development.*

2011b. "China in Africa: What Can Western Donors Learn?" Oslo: Norfund.

2015. *Will Africa Feed China?* New York and London: Oxford University Press.

2016. "How Chinese Money Is Transforming Africa: It Is Not What You Think." Policy Brief, No. 11, 2016. China-Africa Research Initiative, John Hopkins University.

Braütigam, D., and K. Gallagher. 2014. "Bartering Globalization: China's Commodity-Backed Finance in Africa and Latin America." *Global Policy* 5 (3): 346–352.

Braütigam, D., and X., Tang. 2013. "Going Global in Groups: Structural Transformation and China's Special Economic Zones Overseas." *World Development* 63, November, p. 78–91.

Braütigam, D., and H., Zhang. 2013. "Green Dreams: Myth and Reality in China's Agricultural Investment in Africa." *Third World Quarterly* 34 (9): 1676–1696.

Burnside, C., and D. Dollar. 2000. "Aid, Policies, and Growth." *American Economic Review* 90 (4): 847–868.

Cai, F., D. Yang, and W. Meiyan. 2009. "Employment and Inequality Outcomes in China." Institute of Population and Labour Economics, Chinese Academy of Social Sciences; Paper presented to OECD Conference.

Calderón, C., and L. Servén. 2010a. "Infrastructure and Economic Development in Sub-Saharan Africa." *Journal of African Economies* 19 (suppl. 1): 113–187.

2010b. "Infrastructure in Latin America." Policy Research Working Paper Series 5317, World Bank, Washington, DC.

2014. "Infrastructure and Growth." In S. N. Durlauf and L. E. Blume, eds., *The New Palgrave Dictionary of Economics.* London: Palgrave Macmillan.

Canning, D., and E. Bennathan. 2000. "The Social Rate of Return on Infrastructure Investments." Working Paper 2390, World Bank, Washington, DC.

Carothers, T. and D. De Gramont. 2013. *Development Aid Confronts Politics: The Almost Revolution.* Washington DC: Carnegie Endowment for International Peace.

Chandra, V., J. Y. Lin, and Y. Wang. 2013. "Leading Dragon Phenomenon: New Opportunities for Catch-Up in Low-Income Countries." *Asian Development Review* 30 (1): 52–84.

Chang, H. 2003. *Kicking Away the Ladder: Development Strategy in Historical Perspective.* London: Anthem Press.

Chen, C. 2013. "South-South Cooperation in Infrastructure in Sub-Saharan Africa." Working Paper for ECOSOC, United Nations. Mimeo.

Collier, P. 2007. *The Bottom One Billion.* Oxford University Press. London.

Collier, P., and A. Hoeffler. 2004. "Aid, Policy and Growth in Post-Conflict Societies." *European Economic Review* 48 (5): 1125–1145.

Committee for the Sixty-Year History of the Korean Economy. 2010. *The Korean Economy: Six Decades of Growth and Development: II Industry* (in Korean). Available at: http://www.slideshare.net/gdlnkdis/the-korean-economy-six-decades-of-growth-and-development.

Copper, J. F. 2016. *China's Foreign Aid and Investment Diplomacy: Volume 1, Nature, Scope and Origins.* London: Palgrave MacMillan.

Crocker, D. A. 2008. "Development Ethics, Democracy, and Globalization," Part III in Chatterjee, ed., *Democracy in a Global World.*

Custer, S., Z. Rice, T. Masaki, R. Latourell and B. Parks. 2015. *Listening to Leaders: Which Development Partners Do They Prefer and Why.* Williamsburg, VA: AidData. Available at: http://aiddata.org/sites/default/files/publication_full_2.pdf.

Deaton, A. 2013a. *The Great Escape: Health, Wealth, and the Origins of Inequality.* Princeton, NJ: Princeton University Press.

Deaton, A. 2013b. "Weak States, Poor Countries," Project Syndicate, September. Available at: https://www.project-syndicate.org/commentary/economic-development-requires-effective-governments-by-angus-deaton.

Depew, C. 1895. (ed.), *One Hundred Years of American Commerce 1795–1895.* New York: D. O. Haynes & Co.

Development Initiatives. 2013. *Investments to End Poverty: Real Money, Real Choices, Real Lives.* Bristol: Development Initiatives.

Dinh, H., V. Palmade, V. Chandra, and F. Cossar. 2012. *Light Manufacturing in Africa: Targeted Policies to Enhance Private Investment and Create Jobs.* Washington, DC: World Bank.

Doemeland, D., C. Briceno-Garmendia, A. Farah, and J. Herderschee. 2010. "Mining Concessions-for-Infrastructure: Chinese investment in the Democratic Republic of Congo (DRC)." Unpublished. Washington, DC: World Bank.

Easterly, W. 2001. *The Elusive Quest for Growth: Economists' Adventures and Misadventures in the Tropics.* Cambridge, MA: MIT Press.

2003. "Can Foreign Aid Buy Growth?" *Journal of Economic Perspectives* 17 (3): 23–48.

2006. *The White Man's Burden: Why the West's Effort to Aid the Rest Have Done So Much Ill and So Little Good.* New York: Penguin Group.

2013. *The Tyranny of Experts: Economists, Dictators, and the Forgotten Rights of the Poor.* New York: Basic Books.

Easterly, W., R. Levine, and D. Roodman. 2003. "New Data, New Doubts: A Comment on Burnside and Dollar's Aid, Policies and Growth (2000)." Working Paper 9846, National Bureau for Economic Research, Cambridge, MA.

2004. "Aid, Policies, and Growth: Comment." *American Economic Review* 94 (3): 774–80.

Economist Corporate Network. 2015. "China by Far the Largest Investor in African Infrastructure." *Financial Times*, November 30.

Edwards, S. N. 2014a. "Economic Development and the Effectiveness of Foreign Aid: A Historical Perspective." NBER Working Paper 20685, National Bureau for Economic Research, Cambridge, MA.

2014b. *Toxic Aid: Economic Collapse and Recovery in Tanzania.* Oxford: Oxford University Press.

EIB. 2009. *EU-Africa Infrastructure Trust Fund: Annual Report 2009.* Luxembourg: European Investment Bank. Available at: http://www.eib.org/infocentre/pub lications/all/eu-africa-infrastructure-trust-fund-annual-report-2009.htm.

Estache, A. 2003. "Argentina Privatization: A Cure or a Disease?" In C. von Hirschhausen, ed., *Proceedings of a Workshop on Applied Infrastructure Research.* Forthcoming.

2011. *Infrastructure Finance in Developing Countries: An Overview.* Brussels: European Investment Bank.

Estache, A., V. Foster and Q. Wodon. 2002. *Accounting for Poverty in Infrastructure Reform – Learning from Latin America's Experience.* Washington, DC: World Bank.

Farole, T., and G. Akinci. 2011. *Special Economic Zones: Progress, Emerging Challenges, and Future Directions.* Washington, DC: World Bank.

Felipe, J. 2015. *Development and Modern Industrial Policy in Practice: Issues and Country Experiences.* Asian Development Bank and EE Elgar.

Feng, S. 2010. "Mali Sugar Conglomerate CLETC Project Case in Mali." International Poverty Reduction Center in China and Organisation for Economic Co-Operation and Development. Available at: www.iprcc.org.cn /userfiles/file/Feng%20Sheyong-EN.pdf.

Fine, B. 2011, "Locating the Developmental State and Industrial and Social Policy after the Crisis." Background Paper to *The Least Developed Countries Report 2011: The Potential Role of South-South Cooperation for Inclusive and Sustainable Development.* Available at: http://unctad.org/sections/ldc_dir/docs/ldcr2011_ Fine_en.pdf.

Fofack, H. 2014. "The Idea of Economic Development: Views from Africa." UNU-WIDER Working Paper 2014/093, United Nations University, World Institute for Development Economics Research, Helsinki.

Foster, M., and T. Killick. 2006. "What Would Doubling Aid Do for Macroeconomic Management in Africa: A Synthesis Paper." ODI Working Paper 264, Overseas Development Institute, London.

Foster, V., and C. Briceno-Garmendia. 2010. *Africa's Infrastructure: A Time for Transformation*. Washington, DC: World Bank.

Foster, V., W. Butterfield, C. Chen, and N. Pushak. 2009. *Building Bridges: China's Growing Role as Infrastructure Financier for Sub-Saharan Africa*. Washington, DC: World Bank. Available at: https://openknowledge.worldbank.org/bit stream/handle/10986/2614/480910PUB0Buil101OFFICIAL0USE0ONLY1 .pdf?sequence=1.

Freeman, C. 2012. "From 'Blood Transfusion' to 'Harmonious Development': The Political Economy of Fiscal Allocations to China's Ethnic Regions." *Journal of Current Chinese Affairs* 41: 22–23.

Furukawa, M. 2014. "Management of the International Development Aid System and the Creation of Political Space for China: The Case of Tanzania." Research Paper 82, Japan International Cooperation Agency, Tokyo. Available at: https:// jica-ri.jica.go.jp/publication/assets/JICA-RI_WP_No.82.pdf.

G20 Summit, China. 2016. Available at www.g20.org/English/Dynamic/201512/ P020151201039444963631.pdf.

Galiani, S., S. Knack, L. C. Xu, and B. Zou. 2016. "The Effect of Aid on Growth: Evidence from a Quasi-Experiment." NBER Working Paper No. 22164. Cambridge, MA.

Gallagher, K. 2016. *The China Triangle: Latin America's China Boom and The Fate of the Washington Consensus*. London: Oxford University Press.

Gallagher, K., and M. Myers. 2014. "China-Latin America Finance Database." Washington, DC: Inter-American Dialogue. Available at: www.thedialogue .org/map_list.

Gerschenkron, A. 1962. *Economic Backwardness in Historical Perspective*. Cambridge, MA: Belknap Press of Harvard University Press.

Gill, I., and H. Kharas. 2007. "*An East Asian Renaissance: Ideas for Economic Growth.*" Washington, DC: World Bank.

Gransow, B., and Z. Hong. 2009. "China and International Donors: Analysis of Development Management in China." Background paper prepared for the China-DAC Study Group on October 28–29 2009 (Section II).

Greenwald, B. C., and J. E. Stiglitz. 1986. "Externalities in Economics with Imperfect Information and Incomplete Markets." *Quarterly Journal of Economics* 1 (2): 229–264.

Greenwald, B. C., and J. E. Stiglitz. 2014a. "Industrial Policies, the Creation of a Learning Society, and Economic Development." In J. E. Stiglitz, J. Y. Lin, and

E. Patel, eds., *The Industrial Policy Revolution I: The Role of Government Beyond Ideology.* New York: Palgrave Macmillan.

Guo, X. 2009. "Development Experiences of China's Transport Infrastructure." Working paper commissioned by World Bank Institute for China-Africa Experience Sharing Program, co-organized by the Government of China and the World Bank.

Harrison, A., and Rodríguez-Clare, A. 2010. "Trade, Foreign Investment, and Industrial Policy for Developing Countries." In D. Rodrik, ed., *Handbook of Economic Growth vol. 5.*

Hausmann, R. 2013. "The Tacit Knowledge Economy." *Project Syndicate,* October 30. Available at: http://www.project-syndicate.org/commentary/ricardo-hausmann-on-the-mental-sources-of-productivity-growth.

Hausmann, R., J. Hwang, and D. Rodrik. 2007. "What You Export Matters." *Journal of Economic Growth* 12 (1): 1–25.

Hausmann, R., and B. Klinger. 2006. "Structural Transformation and Patterns of Comparative Advantage in the Product Space." Working Paper 128, Center for International Development at Harvard University, Cambridge, MA.

Hausmann, R., D. Rodrik, and A. Velasco. 2005. "Growth Diagnostics." Manuscript, Inter-American Development Bank.

Hidalgo, C., B. Klinger, A.L. Barabasi and R. Hausmann. 2007. "The Product Space Conditions the Development of Nations." *Science* 317 (5837): 482–487.

H.M. Treasury. 2002: *Reforming Britain's Economic and Financial Policy.* London.

H.M. Treasury. 2004: *Long-Term Public Finance Report: An Analysis of Fiscal Sustainability.* London.

Huang, Y., and T. Jiang. 2010. "What Does the Lewis Turning Point Mean for China: A Computable General Equilibrium Analysis." CCER Working Paper E2010005. Beijing: Peking University.

Hynes, W., and S. Scott. 2013. "The Evolution of Official Development Assistance: Achievements, Criticism and a Way Forward." OECD Development Co-operation Working Paper 12, OECD Publishing, Paris, France.

IEO (Independent Evaluation Office) of the IMF. 2007. *The IMF and Aid to Sub-Saharan Africa.* Washington, DC: IMF.

2015. *The IMF's Approach to Capital Account Liberalization: Revisiting the 2005 IEO Evaluation.* Washington, DC: IMF.

IHA (International Hydropower Association). 2013. "Country Profile: China." In *IHA Hydropower Report.* Beijing: IHA China Office.

IMF (International Monetary Fund). 2013. *Regional Economic Outlook: Sub-Saharan Africa – Keeping the Pace.* Washington, DC: IMF.

2014. *The IMF Concludes the Article IV Consultation with Ecuador.* Washington, DC: IMF. Available at: https://www.imf.org/external/np/sec/pr/2014/pr14393.htm.

2014. *World Economic Outlook.* Washington, DC: IMF.

2015. *World Economic Outlook.* Washington, DC: IMF.

IMF and World Bank. 2012. *Revisiting the Debt Sustainability Framework for Low-Income Countries.* Washington, DC: IMF and World Bank.

Ito, T. 1992. *The Japanese Economy.* Cambridge, MA: MIT Press.

Jin, Z. 2012. "China's Marshall Plan – A Discussion on China's Overseas Infrastructure Investment Strategy." *International Economic Review* 2012–06 (in Chinese): 57–64.

Ju, J., J. Y. Lin, and Y. Wang. 2011. "Endowment Structures, Industrial Dynamics, and Economic Growth." Policy Research Working Paper Series 5055, World Bank, Washington, DC.

Kapoor, S. 2013. "Investing for the Future: Good for Norway – Good for Development. Re-Define and National Church Aid (NCA)." Discussion Paper 01/2013. Available at: http://re-define.org/sites/default/files/sites/default/files/images/ReDefineReportonNorwaySWF.pdf

Khor, M. 2015. "China's New South-South Funds: A Global Game Changer?" *IPSNEWs.* November 16. Available at: http://www.ipsnews.net/2015/11/opinion-chinas-new-south-south-funds-a-global-game-changer/.

King, K. 2013. *China's Aid and Soft Power in Africa: The Case of Education and Training.* James Currey, Rochester, NY.

Kissinger, H. 2011. *On China.* New York: Penguin Books.

Kitano, N. 2004. "Japanese Contribution in Supporting China's Reforms: A Study Based on ODA Loans." *China Report* 40 (4): 461–488.

Kitano, N., and Y. Harada. 2014. "Estimating China's Foreign Aid 2001–2013: Comparative Study on Development Cooperation Strategies: Focusing on G-20 Emerging Economies." JICA Research Institute Working Paper 78, Japan International Cooperation Agency, Tokyo.

Koopman, R., Z. Wang, and S.-J. Wei. 2008. "How Much of Chinese Export Is Really Made in China: Assessing Domestic Value-Added When Processing Is Trade Pervasive." NBER Working Paper 14109, National Bureau of Economic Research, Cambridge, MA.

KPMG. 2014. *Infrastructure in China: Sustaining Quality Growth.* Hong Kong: KPMG International.

Krueger, A. O. 1997. "Korean Industry and Trade over Fifty Years." In D. S. Cha, K. S. Kim, and D. H. Perkins, eds., *The Korean Economy 1945–1995: Performance and Vision for the 21st Century.* Seoul: Korea Development Institute.

Krugman, P. 1991. "Increasing Returns and Economic Geography." *Journal of Political Economy* 99 (3): 483–499.

Krugman, P., and A. J. Vernables. 1995. "The Seamless World: A Spatial Model of International Specialization." NBER Working Paper 5220, National Bureau for Economic Research, Cambridge, MA.

Kumar, N. 2008. "South-South and Triangular Cooperation in Asia-Pacific: Towards a New Paradigm in Development Cooperation." Paper presented as a keynote address at the Asia-Pacific Development Cooperation Forum: Regional Workshop on Trends and Progress in Triangular and South-South Cooperation, Bangkok, October 21–22, 2008. Available at: www.un.org/en/ecosoc/newfunct/pdf/backgroundstudy final.pdf.

Kuznets, S. 1930. *Secular Movements in Production and Prices*. New York: Houghton Mifflin Company.

———. 1966. *Modern Economic Growth: Rate, Structure and Spread*. New Haven, CT: Yale University Press.

Li, R. 2007. "A Proper Understanding of Debt Sustainability of Developing Countries." *World Economics and Politics* 4: 63–73.

Li, X. 2013. *International Development Assistance of Non-OECD/DAC Countries*. (in Chinese). Beijing: World Knowledge Publishing House.

Lieberthal, K. 2003. *Governing China: From Revolution Through Reform*. London: W.W. Norton & Company.

Lim, W. 2011. "Joint Discovery and Upgrading of Comparative Advantage: Lessons from Korea's Development Experience." In S. Fardoust, Y. Kim, and C. Sepúlveda, eds., *Postcrisis Growth and Development: A Development Agenda for the G-20*. Washington, DC: World Bank.

Lin, J. Y. 1992. "Rural Reforms and Agricultural Growth in China." *American Economic Review* 82 (1): 34–51.

———. 1995. "The Needham Puzzle: Why the Industrial Revolution Did Not Originate in China." *Economic Development and Cultural Change* 43 (2): 269–292.

———. 2009a. "Beyond Keynesianism: The Necessity of a Globally Coordinated Solution." *Harvard International Review* 31 (2): 14–17.

———. 2009b. *Economic Development and Transition: Thought, Strategy, and Viability*. Cambridge: Cambridge University Press.

———. 2010. "New Structural Economics: A Framework for Rethinking Development." Policy Research Working Paper 5197, World Bank, Washington, DC.

———. 2011a. "A Pro-Growth Response to the Crisis," *Intereconomics: Review of European Economic Policy* 46 (6): 321–326.

———. 2011b. "Global Crisis Requires Global Solutions." Speech prepared for the Council on Foreign Relations, New York (February 28).

———. 2011c. "Growth Identification and Facilitation: The Role of the State in the Dynamics of Structural Change." *Development Policy Review* 29 (3): 264–290.

———. 2011d. "New Structural Economics: A Framework for Rethinking Development." *World Bank Research Observer* 26 (2): 193–221.

———. 2012a. "Building Infrastructure for a Brighter Future: How Infrastructure Investment Initiative Can Generate Growth and Create Jobs in the Developed World." *Foreign Policy*.

———. 2012b. *Demystifying the Chinese Economy*. Cambridge: Cambridge University Press.

2012c. "From Flying Geese to Leading Dragons: New Opportunities and Strategies for Structural Transformation in Developing Countries." *Global Policy* 3 (4): 397–409.

2012d. *New Structural Economics: A Framework for Rethinking Development and Policy*. Washington, DC: World Bank.

2012e. *The Quest for Prosperity: How Developing Economies Can Take Off*. Princeton, NJ: Princeton University Press.

2013. *Against the Consensus: Reflections on the Great Recession*. Cambridge: Cambridge University Press.

2015a. "China's Rise and Structural Transformation in Africa: Ideas and Opportunities." In J. Y. Lin and C. Monga, eds., *The Oxford Handbook of Africa and Economics*. Oxford: Oxford University Press.

2015b. "The Washington Consensus Revisited: A New Structural Economics Perspective." *Journal of Economic Policy Reform* 18 (2): 96–113, doi: 10.1080/17487870.2014.936439.

2015c. "Why I Do Not Support Complete Capital Account Liberalization." *China Economic Journal* 8 (1): 86–93, doi: 10.1080/17538963.2015.1002178.

2016. "Later Comer Advantages and Disadvantages: A New Structural Economics Perspective", in M. Andersson and T. Axelsson, eds., *Can Poor Countries Catch Up*. Oxford: Oxford University Press.

Lin, J. Y., F. Cai, and Z. Li. 1996. *The China Miracle: Development Strategy and Economic Reform*. Hong Kong: Chinese University Press.

Lin, J. Y., and H.-J. Chang. 2009. "DPR Debate: Should Industrial Policy in Developing Countries Conform to Comparative Advantage or Defy It? A Debate Between Justin Lin and Ha-Joon Chang." *Development Policy Review* 27 (5): 483–502.

Lin, J. Y., and D. Doemerland. 2012. "Beyond Keynesianism: Global Infrastructure Investments in Times of Crisis." *Journal of International Commerce, Economics and Policy* 3 (3): 1–29.

Lin, J. Y., and C. Monga. 2011. "Growth Identification and Facilitation: The Role of the State in the Dynamics of Structural Change." *Development Policy Review* 29 (3): 264–90.

Lin, J. Y., and C. Monga. 2012. "The Growth Report and New Structural Economics." In J. Y. Lin, *New Structural Economics: A Framework for Rethinking Development and Policy*. Washington, DC: World Bank.

Lin, J. Y., and D. Rosenblat. 2012. "Shifting Patterns of Economic Growth and Rethinking Development." *Journal of Economic Policy Reform* 15 (3): 171–194.

Lin, J. Y., and G. Tan. 1999. "Policy Burdens, Accountability, and Soft Budget Constraints." *American Economic Review* 89 (2): 426–31.

Lin, J. Y., and Y. Wang. 2008. "China's Integration with the World: Development as a Process of Learning and Industrial Upgrading." World Bank Policy Working Paper 4799, World Bank, Washington, DC.

2013. "Beyond the Marshall Plan: A Global Structural Transformation Fund." Paper for the United Nations Post-2015 High Level Panel on Development Agenda. May 22. Available at: http://www.post2015hlp.org/wp-content/uploads/2013/05/Lin-Wang_Beyond-the-Marshall-Plan-A-Global-Structural-Transformation-Fund.pdf

2014. "China-Africa Cooperation in Structural Transformation: Ideas, Opportunities and Finances." Working Paper 2014/046, United Nations University World Institute for Development Economics Research, Helsinki. Available at: www.wider.unu.edu/publications/working-papers/2014/en_GB/wp2014-046/.

2015. "China and Africa Cooperation in Structural Transformation." In J. Y. Lin and C. Monga, eds. *The Oxford Handbook of Africa and Economics*. Oxford: Oxford University Press.

Lipsey, R. E., E. Ramstetter, and M. Blomstrom. 2000. "Outward FDI and Apparent Exports and Employment: Japan, the US, and Sweden." NBER Working Paper 7623, National Bureau of Economic Research, Cambridge, MA.

Maddison, A. 2001. *The World Economy: A Millennial Perspective*. Paris: OECD Development Centre.

2007. *Chinese Economic Performance in the Long Run – Second Edition, Revised and Updated: 960–2030 AD*. Paris: OECD Development Centre.

2010. Historical Statistics of the World Economy: 1 – 2008 AD. Available at: (www.ggdc.net/maddison/historical_Statistics/vertical-file_02-2010.xls).

Manji, F., and S. Naidu. 2009. "The African Perspective on the Kinds of Development Partnerships China Is Forming in Africa." Paper presented at the China-DAC Study Group "Development Partnership for Growth and Poverty Reduction," October 28–29.

Martens, B., U. Mummert, P. Murrell, and P. Seabright. 2002. *The Institutional Economics of Foreign Aid*. Cambridge and New York: Cambridge University Press.

Mazzucato, M. 2011. *The Entrepreneurial State: Debunking Public Vs. Private Sector Myths*. London: Demos.

McMillian, M., and D. Rodrik. 2011. *Globalization, Structural Change and Productivity Growth*. Cambridge, MA: Kennedy School of Government, Harvard University.

MOF (Ministry of Finance) and World Bank. 2010. *Sharing Knowledge on Development, Promoting Harmony and Progress: 30th Anniversary of the China and World Bank Cooperation*. Beijing: Ministry of Finance.

MOFCOM (Ministry of Commerce of the People's Republic of China). 2009. *A 30-Year History on Development Assistance Cooperation in China*. Beijing: Ministry of Commerce.

2013. *China Africa Economic and Trade Cooperation 2013*. Beijing: Ministry of Commerce. Available at: english.mofcom.gov.cn/article/newsrelease/press/201309/20130900285772.shtml.

Monga, C., and J. Y. Lin. 2015. "Africa's Evolving Economic Frameworks." In J. Y. Lin and C. Monga, eds., *The Oxford Handbook of Africa and Economics*. Oxford: Oxford University Press.

Morrisey, O., and H. White. 1996. "Evaluating the Concessionality of Tied Aid." *The Manchester School* 64 (2): 208–226.

Moyo, D. 2009. *Dead Aid: Why Aid Is Not Working and How There Is a Better Way for Africa*. London: Penguin Books.

Mwase, N., and Y. Yang. 2012. "BRICs Philosophies for Development Financing and Their Implications for LICs." Working Paper WP/12/74, IMF, Washington DC.

Naím, M. 2009. "Rogue Aid." *Foreign Policy*. Available at: http://foreignpolicy.com /2009/10/15/rogue-aid/.

National People's Congress. 2015. *China's 13th Five Year Plan*. (Translation). Available at http://www.npc.gov.cn/npc/zgrdzz/site1/20160429/0021861 abd66188d449902.pdf.

NBS (National Bureau of Statistics of China). 2010. *China Statistical Yearbook*. Beijing: National Bureau of Statistics.

NDRC (National Development and Reform Commission, Department of Foreign Capital and Overseas Investment). 2009. *1979–2005 China's Experience with the Utilization of Foreign Funds*. Beijing: China Planning Press (in Chinese).

New Development Bank. 2014. "Agreements on the New Development Bank," July 15. Available at http://ndbbrics.org/agreement.html.

Nielson, D. L., R. M. Powers, and M. J. Tierney. 2009. "Broad Trends in Foreign Aid: Insights from PLAID 1.6." Working Paper, AidData, Williamsburg, VA. http://s3.amazonaws.com/zanran_storage/irtheoryandpractice.wm.edu /ContentPages/2473385687.pdf

North, D. 1990. *Institutions, Institutional Change and Economic Performance*. Cambridge and New York: Cambridge University Press.

OECD–DAC (Organisation for Economic Co-operation and Development–Development Assistance Committee). 2014a. "High Level Meeting Communiqué, 16 December 2014." Available at: www.oecd.org /dac/OECD%20DAC%20HLM%20Communique.pdf.

———. 2014b. *Modernizing the DAC's Development Finance Statistics*. DOD/DAC (2014) 9, Developing Cooperation Directorate submitted for DAC Senior Level Meeting on March 3–4, 2014, at the OECD Conference Center in Paris, February 17.

———. 2014c. *The Development Cooperation Report 2014: Mobilizing Resources for Sustainable Development*. Paris: OECD Publishing.

OECD. 2016. "TOSSD Compendium" Draft for Discussion. June. Available at http://www.oecd.org/dac/financing-sustainable-development/TOSSD Compendium2016.pdf.

Ollivier, G., J. Sondhi, and N. Zhou. 2014. "High-Speed Railways in China: A Look at Construction Costs." China Transport Topics 9, World Bank, Washington, DC.

Onjala, J. 2008. "A Scoping Study on China-Africa Economic Relations: The Case of Kenya." Available at: http://dspace.africaportal.org/jspui/bitstream/123456789/32023/1/Kenya.pdf?1.

Ostry, J. D., A. R. Ghosh, K. Habermeier, M. Chamon, M. S. Qureshi, and D. B.S. Reinhardt. 2010. "Capital Inflows: The Role of Controls." IMF Staff Position Note SPN10/04, IMF, Washington, DC.

Ostry, J. D., P. Loungani, and D. Furceri. 2016. "Neoliberalism: Oversold?" Finance and Development, June: 38–41.

Ozawa, T. 2004. Institutions, Industrial Upgrading, and Economic Performance in Japan: The "Flying-Geese" Paradigm of Catch-up Growth. Cheltenham: Edward Elgar.

Peterson, G. E. 2008. "Unlocking Land Values to Finance Urban Infrastructure: Land-Based Financing Options for Cities." Trends and Policy Options Series, Public-Private Infrastructure Advisory Facility, Washington, DC.

Prebisch, R. 1950. The Economic Development of Latin America and Its Principal Problems. Reprinted in Economic Bulletin for Latin America 7 (1): 1–22.

Quartey, P., and G. Afful-Mensah. 2015. "Aid to Africa: Emerging Trends and Issues." In C. Monga and J. Y. Lin, eds., The Oxford Handbook of Africa and Economics. Oxford: Oxford University Press.

Rajan, R. G., and A. Subramanian. 2008. "Aid and Growth: What Does the Cross-Country Evidence Really Show?" The Review of Economics and Statistics 90 (4): 643–665.

Ravallion, M., and S. Chen. 2007. "China's (Uneven) Progress Against Poverty." Journal of Development Economics 82 (1): 1–42.

Ray, R., and A. Chimienti. 2015. "A Line in the Equatorial Forests: Chinese Investment and the Environmental and Social Impacts of Extractive Industries in Ecuador." Working Group on Development and Environment in the Americas Discussion Paper 2015-6.

Rodrik, D. 2007. One Economics, Many Recipes: Globalization, Institutions and Economic Growth. Princeton, NJ: Princeton University Press.

Rodrik, D, and M. McMillan. 2010. "Globalization, Structural Change and Productivity Growth." Working Paper 17143, National Bureau of Economic Research, Cambridge, MA.

Roodman, D. 2007. "The Anarchy of Numbers: Aid, Development, and Cross-Country Empirics." World Bank Economic Review 21 (2): 255–77.

Rostow, W. W. 1960. The Stage of Economic Growth: A non-communist manifesto. Cambridge: Cambridge University Press.

Sachs, J. 2009. "Aid Ironies." Huffington Post, May 24. Available at: http://www.huffingtonpost.com/jeffrey-sachs/aid-ironies_b_207181.html.

Samuelson, P. 1954. "The Pure Theory of Public Expenditure." *The Review of Economics and Statistics* 36 (4): 387–389.

Schultze, C. 1983. "Industrial Policy: A Dissent." *Brookings Review* Fall 1983: 3–12.

Sen, A. 1999. *Development as Freedom* (1st ed.). New York: Oxford University Press.

Servén, L. 2007. "Fiscal Rules, Public Investment, and Growth." Policy Research Working Paper 4382, World Bank, Washington DC.

Shen, X. 2015. "Private Chinese Investment in Africa: Myths and Realities." *Development Policy Review* 33 (1): 83–106.

Sheng, A. 2013. "Outlook for Global Development Finance: Excess or Shortage?" Paper prepared for the United Nations Post 2015 HLP on Development Agenda. http://www.post2015hlp.org/wp-content/uploads/2013/06/Sheng_Outlook-for-Global-Development-Finance-Excess-or-Shortage.pdf.

Shimposha, T. K. 2000. "Is Autonomous Development Possible?" In *Globalization of Developing Countries. (Tojokoku no Globalization: Jiritsutechi Hatten wa Kanoka)*. Tokyo: Toyo Keizai Shimposha (in Japanese).

Solow, R. M. 1957. "Technical Change and the Aggregate Production Function." *The Review of Economics and Statistics* 39 (3): 312–320.

State Council Information Office. 2011. "China's Foreign Aid." White Paper, Beijing, April.

——— 2014. "China's Foreign Aid (2010–2012)." White Paper, Beijing, July.

Stiglitz, J. E. 1989. "Imperfect Information in the Product Market." In R. Schmalensee and R. Willig, eds., *Handbook of Industrial Organization vol. 1*. Elsevier.

——— 1996. "Some Lessons from the East Asian Miracle." *World Bank Research Observer* 11 (2): 151–177.

Stiglitz, J. E. 2002. *Globalization and Its Discontents*. New York: W.W. Norton.

Stiglitz, J. E., and B. C. Greenwald. 2014. *Creating a Learning Society: A New Approach to Growth, Development, and Social Progress*. New York: Columbia University Press.

Stiglitz, J. E., and J. Y. Lin. 2013. *The Industrial Policy Revolution I: The Role of Government Beyond Ideology*. New York: Palgrave Macmillan.

Strange, A., B. Parks, M. J. Tierney, A. Fuchs, A. Dreher, and V. Ramachandran. 2013. "China's Development Finance to Africa: A Media-Based Approach to Data Collection." Working Paper 323, Center for Global Development, Washington, DC.

Suh, J. 2007. "Overview of Korea's Development Process until 1997." In J. Suh, and D. H. Chen, eds., *Korea as a Knowledge Economy*. Washington, DC: World Bank.

Summers, L. 2014a. "Invest in Infrastructure That Pays for Itself." *The Washington Post*, October 7. Available at: https://www.washingtonpost.com/opinions/lawrence-summers-invest-in-infrastructure-that-pays-for-itself/2014/10/07/6149d3d6-4ca0-11e4-babe-e91da079cb8a_story.html.

2014b. "U.S. Economic Prospects: Secular Stagnation, Hysteresis, and the Zero Lower Bound." *Business Economics* 49 (2): 65–73.

Sun, H. L. 2011. "Understanding China's Agricultural Investments in Africa." SAIIA Occasional Paper 102.

Sun, Y.-S. 1929. *The International Development of China.* New York: G.P. Putnam's Sons.

Svensson, J. 2003. "Why Conditional Aid Does Not Work and What Can Be Done about It." *Journal of Development Economics* 70: 381–402.

Tang, X. 2014. "The Impact of Asian Investment on Africa's Textile Industries," Carnegie-Tsinghua Center for Global Policy Paper August, Beijing, China.

Temasek Holdings. 2016. Temasek Review 2016. Available at http://www.temasek .com.sg/documents/download/downloads/20160706235822/TR2016_Singles.pdf.

Thomas, V., M. Dailami, A. Dhareshwar, R. E. López, D. Kaufmann, N. Kishor, and Y. Wang. 2000. *The Quality of Growth.* New York: Oxford University Press.

UN Comtrade Statistics. 2015. Available online at http://comtrade.un.org/

UNCTAD Statistics. 2015. *FDI Statistics Division on Investment and Enterprise.* Available at: http://unctad.org/en/Pages/DIAE/FDIStatistics/FDI-Statistics .aspx.

UNIDO (United Nations Industrial Development Organization). 2013. *Industrial Development Report 2013: Sustaining employment growth: the role of manufacturing and structural change.* Vienna: UNIDO.

UNIDO (United Nations Industrial Development Organization) and Peking University. 2015. "Technical Note on the Analytical Framework of GIFUID." UNIDO, Vienna. https://isid.unido.org/files/Senegal/final-technical-note-on-the-analytical-framework-of-gifiud.pdf

UN Office for South-South Cooperation. 2016. "What Is SSC?" Available at: http://ssc.undp.org/content/ssc/about/what_is_ssc.html.

Van der Hoeven, R. 2012. "Development Aid and Employment." Working Paper 2012/17, United Nations University, World Institute for Development Economics Research, Helsinki.

Wang, S., and Y. Ke. 2008. *Concessional Project Financing (BOT, PFI and PPP).* Beijing: Tsinghua University Press (in Chinese).

Wang, Y. 2005. "Development as a Process of Learning and Innovation: Lessons from China." In B. Moreno-Dodson, ed., *Reducing Poverty on a Global Scale.* Washington, DC: World Bank.

2010. "Development Partnership for Growth and Poverty Reduction: A Synthesis." IPRCC Working Paper 7, International Poverty Reduction Center in China, Beijing.

2011a. "Development Partnership." Chapter 1 in *Economic Transformation and Poverty Reduction: How It Happened in China, Helping It Happen in Africa.* China-OECD/DAC Study Group. Available at: http://www.oecd.org/dac/ povertyreduction/49528657.pdf

2011b. "Infrastructure: The Foundation for Growth and Poverty Reduction: A Synthesis." Chapter 3 in *Economic Transformation and Poverty Reduction: How It Happened in China, Helping It Happen in Africa.* China-OECD/DAC Study Group.

Weisbrod, A., and J. Whalley. 2011. "The Contribution of Chinese FDI to Africa's Pre-Crisis Growth Surge." Working Paper 17544, National Bureau for Economic Research, Cambridge, MA.

Williamson, J. 1990. "What Washington Means by Policy Reform." In J. Williamson, ed., *Latin American Adjustment: How Much Has Happened?* Washington, DC: Institute of International Economics.

2002. "Did the Washington Consensus Fail?" Speech at the Center for Strategic and International Studies, Washington, DC, November 6.

Woods, N. (2008). "Whose Aid? Whose Influence? China, Emerging Donors and the Silent Revolution in Development Assistance." *International Affairs* 84 (6), 1205–1221.

Wolf Jr., C., X. Wang, and E. Warner. 2013. *China's Foreign Aid and Government-Sponsored Investment Activities: Scale, Content, Destinations, and Implications.* Santa Monica, CA: RAND National Defense Research Institute.

World Bank. 1987. *Korea Managing the Industrial Transition.* Washington, DC: World Bank.

2008. *The Growth Report: Strategies for Sustained Growth and Inclusive Development.* Washington, DC: World Bank.

2011a. *Chinese investments in Special Economic Zones in Africa: Progress, Challenges and Lessons Learned.* Washington, DC: World Bank.

2011b. "Supporting Infrastructure Development in Low-Income Countries." Submission to the G-20 by the MDB Working Group on Infrastructure, Interim Report, World Bank, Washington, DC.

2011c. *The Changing Wealth of Nations: Measuring Sustainable Development in the New Millennium. Environment and Development.* World Bank Publications, Washington DC. Available at: https://openknowledge.worldbank.org/handle/10986/2252 License: CC BY 3.0 IGO.

2012. *Chinese FDI in Ethiopia.* Washington, DC: World Bank.

2013a. "Financing for Development Post 2015." Staff Report for the Post-2015 Agenda, October.

2013b. *Global Development Horizons: Capital for the Future – Saving and Investment in an Interdependent World.* Washington, DC: World Bank.

2014. *Resource Financed Infrastructure: A Discussion on a New Form of Infrastructure Financing.* Led by H. Halland, J. Beardsworth, B. Land, and J. Schmidt. Washington, DC: World Bank.

2015. *Global Financial Development Report 2015– 16: Long-Term Financing.* Washington, DC: World Bank.

2016. Poverty Overview. Available at http://www.worldbank.org/en/topic/pov erty/overview

Xi, J. 2012. *Washington Post*, February 20.

Xu, J., and R. Carey. 2014. "China's Development Finance: What Issues for Reporting and Monitoring Systems?" *IDS Bulletin* 45 (4).

2015a. "China's Development Finance: Ambition, Impact and Transparency." IDS Policy Brief 353, Institute for Development Studies, Brighton.

2015b. "Towards a Global Reporting System for Development Cooperation on the SDGs: Promoting Transformational Potential and Impact." IDS Working Paper 462, Institute for Development Studies, Brighton.

Yeo, H. K., and G. Akinci. 2011. "Low Carbon, Green Special Economic Zones." In *Special Economic Zones: Progress, Emerging Challenges, and Future Directions*. Washington, DC: World Bank.

Zeng, D. Z. 2010. *Building Engines for Growth and Competitiveness in China*. Washington, DC: World Bank.

2015. "Global Experiences with Special Economic Zones: Focus on China and Africa." Policy Research Working Paper 7240, World Bank, Washington, DC.

Zhou, H., J. Zhang, and M. Zhang. 2015. *Foreign Aid in China*. Beijing: Springer, Heidelberg, and Social Science Academy.

Index